One Small Difference

Step into Action for a Better World

KERRY NELSON

PLACE FOR PEACE PRESS
WOODACRE, CALIFORNIA

Copyright © 2016 by Kerry Nelson

Place for Peace Press
Woodacre, California

LIBRARY OF CONGRESS IN-PUBLICATION DATA
Library of Congress Control Number: 2016941721
Nelson, Kerry
One Small Difference / Kerry Nelson

ISBN
978-0-692-65554-2 (paperback)

Artwork by Anna Oneglia
Book Cover Design by Maragaret Wiley
Interior Book Design by AuthorFriendly.com
Set in Adobe Calson Pro and Century Gothic
PLACE FOR PEACE PRESS
WOODACRE, CALIFORNIA
Printed in the United States of America

"Ours is not the task of fixing the entire world at once, but of stretching out to mend the part of the world that is within our reach."
–Clarissa Pinkola-Estes

"I would have you be a conscious citizen of this terrible and beautiful world."
–Ta-Nehisi Coates

"The prospect really does frighten me that they may finally become so engrossed in a cowardly love of immediate pleasures that their interest in their own future and in that of their descendants may vanish, and that they will prefer to tamely follow the course of their destiny rather than make a sudden energetic effort necessary to set things right."
–Alexis de Tocqueville

Contents

Introduction

When I was a kid my mom gave me a book called *My Book About Me*. In it were spaces for me to write about being Kerry—my favorite colors, friends and family, likes and dislikes, places I'd been, etc. I liked being asked questions about myself; even though it was just a book, I had the comforting feeling that someone was listening to me.

One Small Difference is kind of like *My Book About Me*, only it's focused on your life as one who cares about making a difference in your community. You'll be filling in questions like: Who inspires you? What issues most concern you? As you fill in the blanks, this book will mirror back your unique interests, aspirations, obstacles, supports, and possibilities for engaging in meaningful action.

In large part this book grows out of a "Creative Activism" workshop I created with my friend Joslyn Grieve over a decade ago in Oakland, California. People came to our workshops because they wanted to make a difference. Some wanted to volunteer—with the homeless, with adult learners. Others explored questions: How can I make my business more socially responsible? How can I find the right political group to join up with? Many found answers. Finding the right organization to work with was often the key.

"One small difference" really is all it takes. More than once in conversation with a friend we'd say something like, "Maybe we should start a group." From these initial conversations flowed peace groups, a Green group, a women's support group, a technical solidarity group. Anywhere from three to fifteen people would meet, make leaflets, put on events, plug in computers, stage vigils, go to protests, and share dreams.

Sometimes it takes courage, too—the courage required to face down the inner demons that keep trying to scare us away from taking risks and engaging the issues we care so deeply about.

As you begin, I want to offer three pieces of advice that I think will help you to start and stay engaged, and ultimately make a difference:

- Do something, no matter how small, no matter how brief.
- Connect with at least one other person who wants to engage on the same issue.
- Understand that you are human and that your energy, interest, and abilities to engage will wax and wane over time. Don't try to be the superhuman ideal engager; engage exactly as you are.

EXPLORING ENGAGEMENT

Susan: *I never thought it was possible. I never saw it. It was like an unfulfillable dream.*

Adrienne: *It was like a fantasy.*

Susan: *It was a fantasy. Definitely. There was never a potential. Even now it's almost not a reality. You've got to pinch yourself that it's true—we're living in a free South Africa now.*

Interview with Adrienne Shall and Sue Lieberman in Cape Town, South Africa, in 1997 on "The New South Africa."

WEEK ONE: START

Take that first step

Small Steps Count

"You can do anything if you take a realistic, step-by-step approach. You can't change the whole world, but everybody can do something." –Isao Fujimoto

This is an eight week workbook for people who want to change the world and serve in the world. While many of us talk about wanting to make a difference, this interactive guide will help move you beyond the dinner table conversation and into action.

Maybe you think about volunteering but never make the call. Or you're an activist looking for a group of like-minded citizens, or a parent who is overwhelmed by the climate crisis and looking for some way to respond. This book was written for you if you make statements like, "I want to do something but:"

"I don't have enough time."

"I don't know what to do."

"I need help getting started."

All over the world people contribute to visible positive change just by showing up in the most simple of ways. I once worked with a woman who ran a program removing nonnative plants from Mount Tamalpais in Northern California. The more volunteers she had the more impact they had on controlling the proliferation of these plants. One day she showed me a graph. She said, "See how this year we had so many fewer volunteers? An outsider wouldn't know what accounts for it, but I know that it happened because the man who had managed that volunteer program for fifteen years retired."

You don't need to calculate the value of your labor to know that you have an effect on the world. You just do. Equally important is that you have a heart-based need to confront or assist in a situation that calls to you. You care about the way we are treating the earth, or about people living in poverty, or victims of violence and injustice, or whatever it is that is happening in the world that you feel a need to respond to. Or, you just care about doing the right thing.

Whether your ambitions are simple or grand, this workbook is a space in which you can begin to take action.

How It Works

> *"Small things build up. They make a difference."*
> –Gwenn Craig

The book is divided into three parts: before, during, and after you begin to engage.

In Part One, **Exploring Engagement,** you explore issues and interests, dreams and inspirations, as well as any blocks that are stopping you from engaging. This is both an inner and outer exploration. You'll likely spend time on the Web and talking to people as you look into different options. You'll reflect inwardly on what is most true for you, learning what concerns or situations you are most drawn to address.

In Part Two, **Entering Engagement,** you decide on a project, come up with a plan of action, and take your first steps. The suggestion at this stage is that you hold it lightly. Just try it out.

In Part Three, **Deepening Engagement,** you reflect on your relationship to the larger world. You are invited to speak up, stand up, and give up as practices of bringing yourself into alignment with your values. Can you stretch and "walk your talk" more than you currently do?

In the last chapter, "Reflect," you assess your project (now that you've started), noticing what works, what doesn't, and what adjustments you may need to make. Even though it's "Week Eight," this chapter is intended to be worked with a few weeks or even months after you begin your engagement project.

While the book was designed to help you begin something new, you can also use it to reflect on ways you presently engage in service and change work. You might refresh your perspective, breathe new life into an existing activity, or restart a dormant project.

Your task *this week* is to affirm that you want to do something and make a plan for how you'll work with the workbook over the coming few weeks.

Your Engagement Project

"Engagement project" is a term I came up with to describe whatever action you choose to take to make a difference. The following are all possible engagement projects:

Volunteer with Friends of the Library

Start a blog on immigrant rights

Lower your carbon footprint

Join a political study group

Train to volunteer in the health clinic

Run for a place on your local school board

Begin a search for nonprofit work

For some readers, choosing an engagement project will be easy; you may already have a pretty good idea of what to do and will use this book as a catalyst to move forward. Others will spend more time exploring.

Hold your exploration–and even choice of an engagement project– lightly. In a *One Small Difference* workshop, Howard told the group he had been feeling anxious because he couldn't choose between different project ideas. Then he *got* that he could just take "one small step" and give one of his many interests a try. And if it didn't work out he could try something else. He didn't have to come up with the perfect project in order to get started.

He said, "I realized the one small thing I really want to work with is the video *Alive Inside*." Howard planned to share this film with community groups and spread the word about the remarkably positive impacts of hooking up advanced Alzheimer's patients with their favorite music.

Some Pointers on Working with the Book

You can progress through the book week by week, or you may want to dip into the chapters that are most supportive and interesting to you. For example, if you need inspiration, check out the chapter "Envision." If you've felt frustrated in moving ahead there are some great suggestions for you in the chapter "Unblock."

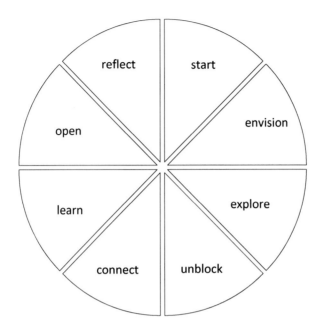

Eight Entry-Points into *One Small Difference*

Consider Buddying Up

While the book was written with the single reader in mind, you may benefit even more if you have a friend to buddy up with, or even a small group that works together. Having others to touch base with each week can enrich your experience and offer motivation. Of course, you'll want to invite people you get along with. All the better if they have somewhat shared interests.

Create a Safe and Respectful Space

Whether you do this workbook alone or with others, it's important that people be able to share thoughts and feelings freely.

Internal safety means you need to lock the door against your own inner critics. Often what discourages us most from acting are our own doubts and negative thoughts about our capacities. Don't let into this process the judges, mothers, fathers, friends, teachers, famous smart people, or anyone else who may be intimidating or not supportive or is saying you should do things their way. Often it is these very voices that have been keeping us from engaging until now.

Group safety requires that you create a supportive group structure. Some ways to do this are:

- Begin each meet-up with a round of check-in. Each person can share a little on how they are doing that day and how their engagement project exploration is coming along.
- Spend five minutes in silence together as a way to let people settle in.
- Establish ground rules for sharing. Have everyone commit to keeping what is said in the group confidential. Never pressure people to share their thoughts or writing if they prefer not to. Consider what you require from the other group members in order to feel both safe and free to say what you need.

Try "Freewriting" Your Answers

"The deepest secret in our heart of hearts is that we are writing because we love the world." –Natalie Goldberg

Many of the exercises in this book are in the form of simple questions, such as:

> **EXERCISE: What can help you work with your blocks?**

If you do the book on your own you'll mostly work with the exercises in written form.

When working with others, you can practice many of the exercises in dialogue, or do a combination of writing and sharing. Don't just *think* about the questions. You will be surprised at how much deeper you can go when you engage through writing or discussion.

If you answer in written form I encourage you to follow these freewriting guidelines:

- Write nonstop, answering whatever question is put to you.
- Decide to write for a set period of time, (e.g. five to ten minutes).
- Allow yourself to veer off topic if that's what happens.
- Try not to edit or cross out during this period.
- Beware of being critical of what you write.
- Keep your pen on the page or your fingers on the keyboard and just keep writing.

A main benefit of this method is that it facilitates free flow of expression; what is revealed when we write freely can have surprising depth and lead to unexpected insights.

Make Time and Make Space

Consider establishing a regular time to do your work with the book, such as one evening a week, or weekday mornings before going to work or school. Choose a time that meshes with a daily or weekly habit. For example, my friend Joslyn found it hard to stick to a daily meditation practice until she came up with the idea of sitting for a few minutes just after brushing her teeth. Remember that you are making time for this because it is a priority for you.

You'll also want to create a space where you can save and refer back to your homework exercises. Perhaps you can set up a folder on your desktop, or buy a notebook.

You may also want to keep a journal or log of your work over the coming weeks. I sometimes use a simple spreadsheet on my laptop to track ideas, activities and reflections, with columns for the "date" and any "notes."

Do Your Homework!

"Muscles function to produce force and cause motion."
—Wikipedia

As much as anything, this is a book of interactive exercises. Just as you build muscles when you go to the gym regularly, your workout with this book will build your engagement muscles—but only if you actually do them.

How thoroughly you engage with the exercises and inquiry is up to you. At the very least you have a map for taking action. If you follow the week-by-week flow of the book, by week five you will be taking your first action steps.

Taking action is great. Even better is showing up in the world in ways that feel impactful and meaningful to you. There are plenty of exercises that guide you into this deeper look at what kinds of engagement will most fulfill you.

That said, you don't need to answer every question. But do at least work with those questions that will most support your exploration and keep you moving along. If you can do this, then the book will work for you. Not only will you start an engagement project, but you may also:

- Gain in confidence to explore and try new things.
- Connect emotionally with the issues you engage and the people you work with.
- Learn new ideas and new ways of seeing.
- Deepen in clarity about what is meaningful and important to you as an engager.

Sasha was in the *One Small Difference* workshop with Howard and that same day she told us about a breakthrough she had when she did an exercise on "speaking up." She said, "I normally avoid speaking out in a way that would be interpreted as remotely controversial. There's fear for me." That week she stepped out of her comfort zone, logged onto Facebook, and posted her view on a current issue, even though doing so made her feel so vulnerable. "I was actually terrified about what was going to happen." As it turned out she said, "A few people heard me and responded and were supportive. Someone said thank you."

Speaking of exercises...

STARTING EXERCISES

1. **What do you hope to get out of your work with this book?** You could articulate this by starting with the statement "I've been wanting to…"

2. **Select an object that can serve as a physical, symbolic reminder of your intention to engage in some way.** This might be a rock, a picture, a plant, etc.

3. **Set aside time to work with this book over the next month or so.** Set aside at least one hour per week and write this in your calendar.

4. **Take one action immediately that relates to the work you want to do with this book.** It can be as simple as calling a friend to say you've decided to do something, or doing a Web search on organizations that work on an area of interest. Take any one first step before heading into the next chapter.

5. **Notice how you feel now that you've expressed your intention to do something.** Does it feel good? Are you a little nervous? Write down any concerns or expectations you have about this decision to act.

6. **Buddy up.** If you have a friend or two who are also going to work with this book, take some time to talk about how you want to check in with one other. Again, you might consider a weekly meeting by phone or in person. Discuss how you can help support one another.

Marcus: *We were all waiting. In the eighties there was this build up: "Free Mandela!" This whole campaign really got going. And we had these massive political marches. So there was this whole expectation that something's going to change within the next few years. Everybody was really tense about it: something will break within the next five years or so. This will not continue for very long.*

Dr. Alan Boesak was a great orator. He carried the struggle in the eighties. The government really suppressed us. They really hammered us. But Alan kept it alive. At university he would make speeches. He was banned—and made speeches. He would always say, "Things are going to change. We are winning this. We are winning this." And that gave us a lot of hope.

Interview with "Marcus" in Cape Town, South Africa in 1997 on "The New South Africa."

WEEK TWO: ENVISION

Explore what moves you

There's a Need

"People have opened their hearts," said Sean Sweeney, who in the days following Hurricane Sandy set up a simple Facebook page to connect storm victims with people who wanted to help. The responses were immediate. A paraplegic man needed a generator, and one was donated within a day. A mother sought clothes and shoes for her kids, and they were given. "It turns out, people really, really want to do something," said Lynn Pentecost, whose agency was given $15,000 in donations for low income families. She said, "They just want to know how to do it."

The desire to show up and contribute to our communities is a reflection of two needs. On the one hand, there's a situation that calls out for our attention: a person needs assistance, a community is in trouble, there's an injustice, a situation of violence, a planet that's heating up. On the other hand, there's you and your need to respond. You want to share what you can—your energy, money, attention. You have the capacity to help. To feel held back from helping can even be painful.

When we participate we satisfy a longing to do what's necessary. We feel fulfilled when we hold a bedridden friend's hand in the hospital, or when we experience the joy of taking part in a rally. It feels right.

This week notice what inspires and motivates you to contribute. Notice how good it feels to think big and dream; how inspiring it can be to join with others; how authentic it feels to "do the right thing," and how grounding it can be to acknowledge your bit part in the big play of our world drama. "All the world's a stage" wrote Shakespeare, and whether you want to be or not, you're in the play.

You Are Moved

Helping those in need is one of the many reasons we initially engage. And maybe this is what's driving you. Or, maybe you're engaging because …

You just have to:

"I can't in good conscience allow the U.S. government to destroy privacy, Internet freedom, and basic liberties for people around the world with this massive surveillance machine they're secretly building."
–Edward Snowden

"I was catapulted into the peace movement with the dropping of the bomb on Hiroshima."
–Ethel Bartol Taylor

"When I found out that 97 percent of the original redwoods had already been cut down, and that the little left was still being destroyed … I knew I had to do something to try to stop it."
–Julia Butterfly Hill

Someone has inspired you:

"Bill Krause would call and say, 'This is not right; look what they're doing,' and by the time I got off the phone it was like, yes what can I do? And I'd drop everything!"
—Gwenn Craig

"[Jackie Robinson] convinced me early on, though he never knew it, that we mustn't aim to do spectacular things – but maybe we will do spectacular things. Instead Jackie Robinson left the impression that we should do what we can, because in the end, by standing up to the bully, you win a little victory for righteousness and you give just one other person the example to stand up for truth."
– Desmond Tutu

You need to live or act in a way that more deeply aligns with your values:

"One day I went to a restaurant in Stellenbosch [South Africa]. And a black guy walked in, who said 'I'm here to buy takeaway.' And I had become political enough to know that he wasn't allowed to eat there—to notice. So I didn't finish my meal. I just went and paid, and by that evening I resolved never to go to an apartheid place again."
—Kallie Hanekom

"I became increasingly uncomfortable about having so much while my brothers and sisters were starving. Finally I had to find another way."
—Peace Pilgrim

You want to make a living doing something that has meaning for you:

"I know it's a cliché, but I really wanted to teach to make a really significant difference and I just love watching the change in the pupils over the year, you watch them grow in confidence and self-belief and all I want is to give them that because it is the biggest catalyst for getting them to learn and grow. I want to bring out the best in them."
—Adam Lopez

"When I got out of college in 1970, I went to work for the Housing Authority in Pittsburgh, a kind of social service job, right? I didn't want to go to graduate school. I wanted to be an activist. I wanted to bring about change."
—Roberta Lynch

You are driven to protect or promote your rights or the rights of others:

"Last month, I participated in a vigil in Madera for the happenings in Oaxaca, Mexico. Oaxaqueños like myself gathered at the Courthouse park as a way of coping with our frustration and pain for what is happening to our people back in our home state. At the vigil we made posters and voiced chants, we also had an open mic for people to speak their minds. I wrote a letter... a call to action for people to stop trying to drive out hate with hate and to come together."
– Brenda Ordaz Garcia

"Residents in one third of California's reservations lacked clean drinking water, and Native Americans here had an average life expectancy of only forty-two years. ... The story was the sort I gravitated toward because it exemplified my determination to give a voice to the voiceless."
–Belva Davis

High school student Malik Curtis attended a Black Lives Matter protest in Minneapolis in 2015. Why? "It's just simple," he said, "Us being oppressed for so many years, and [in] solidarity with Baltimore...I'm with my people, that's pretty much it... I'm just really tired of it. This is the society we live in and hopefully, we can overcome it."

You simply have a great idea that you believe can benefit people:

"About six months after moving to my new home, a huge parcel of land went up for sale," said Buddhist teacher Tempel Smith. *He immediately saw a retreat center there—in a location very accessible to people in the East Bay. The land was beautiful and the price seemed within reach if he could find others who wanted to participate. "I got very inspired. It seemed like if the retreat center were there it would be used."*

In addition to our more altruistic motives, we may want to get involved to make our own lives better. Maybe you just want to connect with others who care about the same causes. Or maybe you want to make new friends or try something new.

"Something taps into my emotions–this is wrong, this is an injustice, somebody's been hurt here," said Gwenn Craig, a long time gay rights activist. "You know if it moves me to tears it motivates me to action."

We act because we need to act, and because we are needed. As the poet Rilke says, "Everything here apparently needs us."

> **EXERCISE: Complete this sentence and take a few minutes to freewrite about this:**
>
> "I need to engage at this time because…"

You Are Inspired

"Every time there's a publicized kidney donation, hospitals field dozens of calls from people who say they're willing to do the same."
—Mark Barasch

People inspire us. We witness a generous, creative, courageous, or selfless act, and we want to do that too. Or someone gives a great speech. We admire them. We want join their cause.

Inspiration can catch fire; a simple, selfless gesture can lead to a proliferation of positive actions by others.

Edward Snowden inspired journalist Glenn Greenwald to risk everything to get out the story of the National Security Agency spying on private citizens. At the Socialism Conference in June 2013, Greenwald expressed awe at Snowden's courage. "Snowden was a high school dropout. He has zero prestige, and yet by himself has literally changed the world. … The choice that he made was so incredibly powerful. I was tremendously inspired myself. I set out–with *The Guardian*–to shake up the foundations of the corrupted and rotted roots of American media and culture."

Groups inspire us. When he was a teenager, Isao Fujimoto entered a lifelong relationship with the nonprofit American Friends Service Committee (AFSC). Isao grew up on an Indian reservation in Yakima, Washington, and later in an internment camp for Japanese-Americans during World War II. It was there he first encountered

AFSC. "When I was in the Heart Mountain Concentration camp in 1942, a young person came to our barracks and said, 'There's a present for you! There are presents for everybody in this camp!' We were completely astounded, you know, because we were in prison. ... AFSC was the only group I know about that went to the camps to help out in all kinds of ways. And one of the most amazing things they did was help the college-aged students get out of the camps and find them a place to continue their education."

Isao said, "One of the first things I did after being discharged from the army is I went to the AFSC office in Japantown in San Francisco, and I said, 'I really appreciate what you've done during the wartime, and I'm willing to put in my time for you.' That was in 1958. Ever since that time I've been involved with them."

Isao went on to become a deeply committed, lifelong community activist and academic in Davis, California. Among his many projects, Isao helped start and chaired the Asian American Studies Department at UC Davis. He took students from Davis on inner-city field trips in San Francisco each year, to expose them to the deep service work being done by local churches and service agencies with the homeless. He opened his own home (his enclosed porch, to be precise) to house several small environmental nonprofits, essentially helping birth environmental programs such as the Davis Farmers Market. Colleague Mark Miller said of Isao, "He doesn't just develop people; he's interested in doing what he can to help them grow. He tries to provide conditions in which they will thrive."

> **EXERCISE: Who inspires you?** Describe a person or group that inspires you. What do they do that you admire? What about them is special or distinct? How would you characterize them?

You Want to Join a Movement

"There comes a time when the operation of the machine becomes too odious, makes you so sick at heart, that you can't take part, you can't even passively take part, and you've got to put your bodies upon the gears and upon the wheels, upon all the apparatus, and you've got to make it stop. And you've got to indicate to the people who run it, the people who own it, that unless you're free, the machine will be prevented from working at all."

–Mario Savio

Movements inspire us. Movements are about change. They try to up-root and shift deeply ingrained patterns of injustice, oppression, and harm. They are the opposite of stasis, apathy, and cynicism. At the center of every movement are people–ultimately lots of people–who give all they can, informing others, lobbying, campaigning, organizing. Hope, patience, certainty, dedication, and determination fuel them. It takes a lot of people saying "this is not right" or "this way would be better" to give birth to a movement and keep it going.

Twenty-first-century movements include Black Lives Matter, OCCUPY, Arab Spring, living wage, immigrant rights, and climate action, to name a few. Twentieth-century social movements are largely responsible for voting rights for women, African Americans, and native Americans; for ending the Vietnam War, and checks on nuclear proliferation.

When South End Press asked Michael Albert, editor of the progressive *Z Magazine*, "What achievements of the Left have given you the most hope for the future?" he answered, "Ending feudalism, ending slavery, enacting labor laws, winning universal suffrage, ending Jim Crow laws, overcoming much of the mindset and practice of patriarchy as it was entrenched throughout the '50s and '60s, bringing gay rights and libera-tion into the light of social policy and practice, and putting ecology on the political map. The Left has had a long lineage."

We join movements because they really are "by the people" and "for the people" and we want to contribute and take part. Movements can have profound impacts on our lives. If you're a U.S. citizen, consider how your own life would be different were it not for movements like civil rights, women's rights, and gay rights.

In September 2014, I rode with Bing Gong on the "People's Climate Train" from California to join the People's Climate March in New York City. About 150 activists held a four-day-long, continual conversation on the train, sharing information, strategies, and ideas on how to address the climate crisis. Bing produces and co-hosts the show Post-Carbon Radio, and works for the International Forum on Globalization. As we watched the Colorado River winding alongside the train he said, "It's pretty exciting being with other allies and passionate people who are working hard to fight the destruction of the tar sands, even laying down their bodies to stop the machinery. It gets pretty discouraging sometimes fighting the forces, but that's why I go to this protest in solidarity with friends and people who feel the way I do. We're here to stop the destructive forces that are causing ecological collapse."

When we reached New York and joined the People's Climate March a few days later, the 100,000 who were expected had blossomed into 400,000. Manhattan was a sea of diverse, determined, committed people of all ages, from all parts of the country and the world, saying that the planet was worth saving and the political and corporate apathy in the face of the crisis had to end.

> **EXERCISE: Appreciate movements.** Which social movements are you most grateful for and why? Are there any you feel passionate about? How have any of these movements especially impacted your own life or the lives of people in your community? Have you been part of movements? Have you ever thought of joining a movement?

Animal Rights	Anti-Apartheid
Arab Spring	Anti-Nuclear
Civil Rights	Anti-Colonial
Black Consciousness	Anti-War
Disability Rights	Environment
Farm Worker	Free Speech
Indigenous Peoples	Labor
LGBTQ Rights	Occupy
Pro Choice	Women's Rights

You Need to Do the Right Thing

"I used to feel that I had to be good, truly good in my heart and spirit, in order to do good. But it's the other way around: if you do good, you become better."
–Zell Kravinsky

"Disinterested concern for others, and the rejection of every form of self-centeredness and self-absorption, are essential if we truly wish to care for our brothers and sisters and for the natural environment. ... If we can overcome individualism, we will truly be able to develop a different lifestyle and bring about significant changes in society."–Pope Francis

Your engagement may be driven by the need to do the right thing. To walk your talk. To align your actions with your more deeply held beliefs. Values and beliefs inform our political affiliations, our purchases, and our behavior.

Opportunities to align our actions with our beliefs abound. Believe in human rights? Then don't buy products made in factories that employ children or pay starvation wages. Believe in kindness? Let others go first in line at the grocery store, or let that car signaling you on the freeway cut in front of you. Believe in changing the system? Then join an organization that is trying to make that happen.

As the Sri Lankan leader of the Sarvodaya movement, Dr. A. T. Ariyaratne, said, "If you think something is right, do it." And Highlander Education Center's founder Myles Horton put it, "Neutrality is just another word for accepting the status quo as universal law. You either choose to go along with the way things are, or you reject the status quo. Then you're forced to think through what you believe."

South African Pramod Daya, who as a young man loved science and physics and playing guitar, saw no other choice than to be an activist at university in the seventies. In a different situation Pramod might not have become politically active, but he said he felt a "moral necessity" to engage. "You were so privileged to be at university: you had access to resources and money and that kind of stuff that gave you an education. … And things were so severe and dire in this country. So if you had any kind of emotional content at all in your makeup, you just kind of had to take on the responsibility of being involved in social activism to change the way the world was because things were extremely bad."

You'll take a closer look at beliefs in Week Seven. In the meantime, consider how central your values and beliefs are in your life. Do you hold them tightly or more lightly? Which do you most cherish?

EXERCISE: Take some time to reflect on which beliefs and values are driving your engagement. Consider what you believe in and *how important those beliefs are to you*. Especially consider which beliefs are the most important. Which beliefs especially guide you in your daily life and in interactions with others? Write or dialogue with others about this. Here are some possibilities:

Caring for others	Human rights
Justice	Freedom
Teaching and Sharing	Alleviating suffering
Practicing what you preach	Speaking truth to power
Integrity	Courage

You Feel Responsible

"We all face a choice. We can ignore the problems that lie just beyond our front doors… We can yell at the TV newscasters and complain about how bad things are… or we can work, as well as we can, to shape a more generous common future." –Michael Lerner

"If you don't like the news, go out and make some of your own." –Wes Nisker

One of the main drivers in our desire to make a difference is also one of the easiest to overlook, and that is that we *are* the news. We want to contribute to solutions for the world because it's our world. We are the people we keep reading about in newspapers and on our smartphones. We're in the business, politics, science, and culture sections, and on the front page.

We are in a relationship with the world. The Random House Dictionary defines "world" as "the earth with its inhabitants and all things upon it," and "relation" as "a significant association" or "connection."

We have a significant connection to the earth itself. This is obvious: no earth, no people. Take the earth away and the people go cartwheeling off into outer space. The earth is what connects us all.

We have a significant association with all of humanity, and to all life on earth. What each of us does (or does not do) affects not only ourselves and our family and friends, but also humanity and other living beings on the earth in subtle ways we can never wholly understand. But we do affect one another.

I used to ask people I interviewed how they felt about being American. Isao's response was: "Lots of things are possible here. But things don't happen automatically. People really have to contribute, rather than just criticize or leave things alone."

To be in relationship with our country and our world means we share in the responsibility for taking care of the communities we are part of. We are involved whether we choose to contribute or not.

I love doing the following exercise every now and then because it reminds me that while I often feel disconnected when reading or listening to the news, if I take time to reflect on a piece, I almost always notice ways in which the article connects directly to my life or to the lives of people I know.

> **EXERCISE: Read a short article on a topic of interest or concern and spend some time writing and reflecting about your reading experience.** Consider if this article has any direct impact on your life or on the lives of people you know. Notice that even an "impersonal" news article connects to your own life. After reading you might review it in light of these questions:
>
> What did you learn?
>
> Who is impacted by this situation?
>
> Are there "winners" and "losers"? Who are they?
>
> Does anything about the article confuse you?
>
> Is this something you want to share with others? If yes, why?

You Care

"We all secretly know that giving is the only way to fill up, that it's the only way home." –Anne Lamott

"All the great movements for social justice in our society have strongly emphasized a love ethic." –bell hooks

Love moves us. We are moved to act out of compassion, concern, kindness, the desire to share, give, nurture, and heal. We want to make people happy. In my workshops, participants share ways they want to care for the world. One man said: "I wish I could give the earth commitment and care from all of humanity." Another expressed a desire "to help kids cultivate their love and caring for those around them." A young Buddhist wanted to share her love of the Buddhist teachings with others.

Throughout her book *A Paradise Built in Hell*, Rebecca Solnit makes the point that at times of disasters like 9/11 and Hurricane Katrina, "most people are altruistic, urgently engaged in caring for themselves and those around them, strangers and neighbors as well as friends and loved ones."

Solnit shared Temma Kaplan's story of this phenomenon. Kaplan, who was in New York during 9/11, recalled that on that day "everybody wanted to respond. I went back to my block, and some of my neighbors were on a street corner raising money; we didn't know what for but they thought that people would need things, and so they started raising money. … I felt that everybody was holding on to each other in order to try and brace and embrace each other. … For a short time during the first few days after 9/11, I felt that 'beloved community' that we talked about in the Civil Rights Movement."

There's the desire to help and heal, and then there's just the simple kindnesses we extend whether with purpose or automatically throughout the day. "Practice random acts of kindness and beauty" was a bumper sticker showing up a lot in the San Francisco Bay Area many years ago. Around that time more than one friend relayed stories of strangers in the cars in front of them paying for their bridge tolls.

Compassion moves us. Gestures of compassion are as simple as offering money to a homeless person, or as dramatic as tying oneself to a bulldozer in an act of civil disobedience. In the book Compassion in Action, Ram Dass wrote, "During the moments I was in ecstatic states of consciousness, I recognized the innate generosity of my heart and the ease with which one could merge with another's suffering in such a way as to experience it not as her or his suffering but as 'our' or 'the' suffering."

> **EXERCISE: Name any person, social group, species, or place that especially needs to be cared for at this time.**
>
> What feelings arise for you around this being or situation and what actions, gestures, or resources could help them? What gifts might you have to offer?

You Dream

"In our acts of goodness and conviction we are planting shade trees for grandchildren who have not yet been born."
–Anne Lamott

"We must cultivate the capacity to imagine a world other than the one of injustice, war, and environmental destruction. But we must also carefully differentiate imagination from fantasy."
–Larry Robinson

At the heart of every desire to contribute there resides an idea of what could be. It's a big dream, a best-case scenario. It is what we reach for.

We all dream. Even if we don't believe the fairytale ending will come about, we still want it to. We want them to get married at the end of the story. We want the good people to win. Or the good part of ourselves.

The dreamer is often depicted as the one with her head in the clouds, unconcerned with reality, lost in pretty ideas. But the biggest dreamers I've known are nothing like that. Most are pragmatic, determined, willing to give up evenings and weekends for a cause or a person they care about.

As kids we're encouraged to dream. As adults we are often asked to come up with goals. In our workplaces dreams show up in mission statements:

"We nurture the faith that conflicts can be resolved nonviolently, that enmity can be transformed into friendship, strife into cooperation, poverty into wellbeing, and injustice into dignity and participation. We believe that ultimately goodness can prevail over evil, and oppression in all its many forms can give way." —American Friends Service Committee

"We therefore are determined not to support any kind of war, international or civil, and to strive nonviolently for the removal of all causes of war." —War Resisters League

Andrew Nyathi and his comrades dreamed of a free Zimbabwe. In the 1970s in southern Rhodesia (now Zimbabwe), Andrew, along with thousands of others, fought for the liberation of his people from colonial rule. Zimbabwe became independent in 1980, at which point Andrew began putting his energies into building a worker cooperative, and later towards helping grow a cooperative movement in Zimbabwe.

As Andrew and his fellow workers set about creating their cooperative, they held meetings to talk about what they were trying to create. They started by talking about their belief in freedom. "We tried to list all of the things we meant by freedom. Obviously we meant political freedom– the freedom to be governed through elected representatives of our own choice. But we also meant social freedom–freedom from racist oppression, the freedom to talk and associate as we wished. And–here the discussion became particularly animated–freedom, we insisted, meant above all economic freedom: the freedom to eat good food; freedom to live in comfort; the freedom to produce the way we wanted to produce.

"A vision unfolded before our eyes. We saw before us not only our own co-op but a whole society organized along co-operative lines–a cooperative Zimbabwe with a government sensitive to the problems of coops, and banks and financial institutions only too anxious to help. We saw a free Zimbabwe which would be able to take its place among the free nations of the world."

An Earth Charter

Another example of big dreaming is the Earth Charter. Initiated by the United Nations in the 1990s, thousands of people representing civil society organizations and governments across the globe engaged in five years of discussion and consultation to create the Charter, which was completed in January 2000.

The charter comprises sixteen principles for living together on earth including:

- Respect the earth and life in all its diversity.
- Care for the community of life with understanding, compassion, and love.
- Build democratic societies that are just, participatory, sustainable, and peaceful.
- Secure earth's bounty and beauty for present and future generations.
- Protect and restore the integrity of earth's ecological systems, with special concern for biological diversity and the natural processes that sustain life.

When organizations and citizens articulate their dreams this way, positive things happen. Maybe not immediately, and maybe not in the ways we expect. But we "give peace a chance," as the song reminds us. When we don't recognize our dreams we lose the chance to use our creativity to foster the kind of world we need. If we are afraid to even imagine what a "better" world can be, how can we start to work for it? We need to take our dreams seriously.

EXERCISE: Practice Dreaming for the World. Take any issue (e.g., education, health care, war, poverty) and come up with a best case scenario for how that situation might be greatly improved or resolved. For example if your issue is education, maybe you envision publically funded schools where children get all the support they need: small class sizes, tutors, healthy lunches, libraries, and more. Imagine what it will be like when those changes take place. How will people's lives be different? " My dream for [this issue] is":

ENVISIONING EXERCISES

1. **Many motivators.** Reflect on the different reasons you want to engage. Which motivating factors do you resonate with in the chapter? (The options were: inspired by people or groups or movements, "Do the Right Thing," responsible citizenship, and caring.)

2. **When have you felt inspired in the last year?** Think of any inspiring situation you witnessed or were part of. What were the circumstances? Who was involved? Did this experience motivate you to take action or to share your experience with others?

3. **Appreciate your ancestors.** Describe one event in world history or in your own family history that you are especially grateful for. Something that has had a positive impact on your life. How does it feel to know that that there are people now long gone who have affected your life in this way?

4. **Connect with your great-great-grandchildren.** Imagine you are talking with someone who lives a hundred years from now, maybe a relative or someone who lives where you do today. What would you like or need to tell them about how we are caring for the world today? What do you think they will tell you about their experience? Have an imaginary conversation with this friend from the future. (This exercise is inspired by Joanna Macy's "Audio Recording to the Future" exercise in her book, *Coming Back to Life*.)

5. **Do something good today.** Zell Kravinsky said "If you do good, you become better." Spend a day purposely "doing good" and write about it at the end of the day. You might start with being especially kind to others. Notice what opportunities arise. How did it feel to spend the day this way?

6. **Express what matters most.** What is the one thing in life that is truly important for you to give voice to, express, and share with others? Write this down, taking as long as you need, then share it with someone.

Gwenn: *In 1975 you could come to San Francisco and just immediately get enveloped into the city.*

Dennis: *And you knew that San Francisco was going to be what it was, right? You specifically picked here?*

Gwenn: *Yes! I actually came a little late. (Laughing.) Because some of the things I was looking for were either over or they were ending.*

Kerry: *What were you looking for?*

Gwenn: *Well, the counterculture.*

Dennis: *Drugs, sex, rock and roll.*

Kerry: *Which counterculture?*

Dennis: *Drugs, sex!*

Gwenn: *I wasn't really into politics when I first got here at all. So, more the self-realization stuff.*

Dennis: *Were you out of the closet by then? I was one toe out. 1972. That's when I came here. I always have been at the end, but never at the beginning, of any movement. Like the antiwar thing: I was a little late! I lived on Castro Street. I lived upstairs from Harvey Milk. That was the only movement I've ever been at the beginning of.*

Kerry: *You coincidentally moved upstairs from Harvey Milk?*

Dennis: *Yeah. There was a woman named Margaret. She said—you've got to come up here. There's a political movement, there's a sex movement, there's drugs, there's everything. So about six of us moved. First we lived on Page Street, by the park, then we moved to Castro Street.*

Kerry: *What were the first political activities you got involved in?*

Gwenn: *The first thing that I jumped into rather wholeheartedly was Harvey's '77 campaign. And I was the get out the vote coordinator along with Bill Krause. And it was like, "God, you're political?!" Bill Krause and I were very close friends then. We got to be friends before we realized that both of us had an interest in politics. So that sort of came up... "Oh, you care about that stuff?" – "Oh, you care about that?"*

Dennis: *Counterculture hippies who moved into politics.*

Interview with Dennis Seely and Gwenn Craig in San Francisco, California, in 1999, on "Political Engagement."

WEEK THREE: EXPLORE

Explore what you might do

Many Possibilities

"In the beginner's mind there are many possibilities. In the expert's there are few."
–Suzuki Roshi

Last week you explored what motivates you to engage. This week you explore ideas for your engagement project by spending time with three questions:

What does "making a difference" mean to you?

What kinds of actions can you imagine taking?

What issues are important to you?

After graduating from college in 1987 I drove over the Golden Gate Bridge on a wave of freedom, seeking adventure and a deeper look at America and myself. My plan was to spend a few weeks on the road, choose a city, wait tables for money, and then maybe move on from there.

After a month of highways, youth hostels, truck stops, diners, and a close encounter with a tornado, my 1969 turquoise-blue Toyota Corona and I rolled into New Orleans at dusk. The car died a block away from the Youth Hostel. I had sixty dollars to my name, one of which I gave to the homeless man who helped me push the car into a parking space. Within a week or two I was waiting tables in the French Quarter for $2.13 an hour. Months later I continued on to Mexico, New York, and eventually to Zimbabwe and beyond.

As you explore ways you might engage, let your intuition guide you, and be willing to be surprised. Having a plan is a good way to start, but it's even more interesting when we lose the map or when the car breaks down. As the seventeenth-century Japanese poet Matsuo Bashō wrote, "Every day is a journey and the journey itself is home."

> **EXERCISE: What is one very appealing, but perhaps unlikely, possibility for your engagement project?** Write a paragraph or two on the "pie in the sky" scenario.

At Least Two Roads

"Those who get involved view their place in the world very differently. They have learned specific lessons about approaching social change: that they don't need to wait for the perfect circumstances, the perfect cause, or the perfect level of knowledge to take a stand; that they can proceed step by step, so that they don't get overwhelmed before they start."
–Paul Loeb

There are lots of ways to drive from San Francisco to New Orleans. And there are even more ways to make a difference.

Draw a map in your mind of the round world and the seven continents, and imagine for a moment the millions of people who are working as nurses, teachers, those helping elderly and disabled, those helping the starving, people working in homeless shelters or assisting immigrants, and those counseling people who are out of work. Add to them the millions who work hard for social changes: the union organizers, the community organizers, the human rights advocates and their volunteers, the environmental activists and ecologists and conservationists, the political organizers and politicians trying to make democracies work, the peace marchers, war resisters, mediators, activists, and utopians. And expand this to include mothers and fathers and brothers and sisters who in many little ways each day take care of the kids, the grandparents, the neighbors who can't get around so well. Imagine the bus driver who always smiles, the politician who risks her position as she stands up for her beliefs, and the boy standing up to the bullies in the playground and not giving in, not becoming one of them. Circle through this the zillions of moments of choosing to do good, choosing integrity over advantage, speaking kindly even when angry, or volunteering even a minute or two of our time to help someone else when we are in a hurry.

When we say we want to make a difference or make a better world, we generally mean we either want to take care of other people (or animals or the earth) or we want to change how things are done—improve on the systems for taking care of people, the animals, the earth. I refer to these two roles as "caretakers" and "changemakers."

Both caretakers and changemakers take care of the world, but they go about it from different angles.

> **Caretakers** engage in ways that are nurturing and supportive, often in direct one-on-one relationships with other people. They sit next to hospital beds and hospice beds, tutor kids after school, counsel LGBTQ youth, conserve land, and encourage you to adopt kittens.

> My friend Betsy is a caretaker. She worked for years as a nurse and more recently as a hospice volunteer. I was deeply moved when she shared that she had "no doubt in her being" that she wanted to help people through the dying and grieving process.

> **Sometimes caretakers**: work in shelters and hospices; help people find jobs; work with kids and seniors; provide health, spiritual, and

psychological care; work in refugee camps; work in libraries; help low income communities; conserve wildlife; teach and train.

Changemakers work to change systems or minds. They picket the supermarket to rally for GMO labels, host political films at their homes, campaign for candidates, and run for office.

My friend Jon is a changemaker. Jon has joined many campaigns and causes from the nuclear freeze in the 1980s, to anti-apartheid, to OCCUPY Oakland. He is a consistent presence at demonstrations and encourages others to participate.

Sometimes changemakers: advocate for health care reform; are government officials; track human rights violations; organize and attend protests and rallies; create alternative communities; inspire people to work for change; organize neighbors, coworkers, and other groups that have common concerns; teach and train.

Notice if you lean more towards caretaking or changemaking. Often these roles overlap, like the shelter worker who both counsels the residents and advocates for improved support services. And of course there are other roles too, like the **"ethical engager"** who seeks to align her actions and/or livelihood with her values and beliefs. Vegans, tax resisters, and avid recyclers are examples of ethical engagers.

What's Your Definition?

We use a lot of lingo to talk about this very broad idea of "making a difference." Lingo, while simplistic, can provide some useful shorthand to talk about what we value. I recently told a friend that I tend to be guided by the phrase "do the right thing." He then one-upped me saying he worked with the phrase "do the right *next* thing."

Ultimately what matters is what we personally mean when we talk about "making a difference." See if any of the phrases below connect with you or even guide you as you think about how you want to engage:

Make a better world	Change the world	Do good
Walk your talk	Pay it forward	Politically engage
Donate	Offer charity	Socially engage
Save the world	Help	Speak truth to power
Prevent harm	Offer service	Contribute
Do the right thing		

> **EXERCISE: Consider what you mean when you say you want to "make a difference."** Not that you necessarily say that. But you say something–contribute, help, change things, do the right thing. Write a paragraph beginning with this sentence "For me [making a difference/activism/helping others, etc.] is about...

You Can Help Others

"Our impulses to care for one another often seem instinctive. The more we're able to act on them freely, the more opportunity we have to feel whole and be helpful."
–Ram Dass and Paul Gorman

Jim Bates is all about service. When Jim retired from a career as a remodel contractor in his sixties, he and his wife scaled back. They sold their home in Colorado and relocated to Northern California, where they now work at Spirit Rock Meditation Center (where I also work). Jim works in the Facilities Department and tends the buildings and the land, and Cheryl works in the kitchen. They made this life change as a way to offer service–to give back.

After hours Jim is a hospice volunteer. He described his first assignment, working with "Mr. Jones," a man who had chronic obstructive pulmonary disease and who was "very frail." Jim said, "He can't get out of his chair without help. But he's mentally very present and able to talk about everything and we sit and tell stories."

Jim "helped" Mr. Jones just by being with him and listening. During the hospice training Jim was nervous about what it would be like.

Would he be able to do it–to be with people who were dying? It turned out that hospice work has been unlike anything Jim has ever encountered before. He said, "When you're sitting with somebody who's dying it's different from most of what you've done in your life. And it's an invaluable experience to touch into that part of our life which we do not often look at: death, dying, sickness, and old age."

Being of service is important to Jim. "What's left?" he said. "It's not about career. It's not about raising kids. It's not so much about getting something for us anymore. When you take away all those things that you do for thirty to forty years in your life, what is there left to do besides serve?"

You Can Change the World

"I had no epiphany, no singular revelation, no moment of truth, but a steady accumulation of a thousand slights, a thousand indignities and a thousand unremembered moments produced in me an anger, a rebelliousness, a desire to fight the system that imprisoned my people."
–Nelson Mandela

In 1994, Nelson Rolihlahla Mandela was elected president of South Africa, heralding the end to apartheid. It took nearly a century of organized protest and resistance to bring this about. Over the decades from 1912 onwards, generations of men, women, and youth protested white rule and the oppressive forms it took in all kinds of ways and in every sector of society, usually at risk of being jailed, harassed, beaten, exiled, or killed. They did so never knowing what the impact of their actions would be, or if they themselves would ever live in a "free" South Africa.

"How did you picture post-apartheid South Africa?" I asked a friend who had been active.

"We couldn't conceive the post-apartheid," Anton answered. "Could not."

When I lived in South Africa I met countless people like Anton who helped bring forth the new democracy. Marcus was one. As a child he dreamed of a day when he and his family could go to the movies or shop in the nicer parts of town or not be constrained to shop in the "coloured" sections of stores. (Note that "coloured" is considered an ethnic group in South Africa and not a derogatory term.) Members of his family were politically active, and about growing up he said, "There was always police harassment, and those kinds of things. And all you wished is that this is all over. You know? So we can just get on and live normal, boring lives."

When Marcus went to university he began to dream of political freedom as well. "I wanted to make my own choices, but also not to be bothered by politics anymore." He joined the African National Congress (ANC) in order to fight against the system. He also joined the university's "adventure club," which offered an excellent cover for his role of helping locate politically active youth who ran away into the "bush" with the intention of joining the ANC military wing.

"Somebody would call you and say, 'Four kids have disappeared from Soweto. They were involved in politics. We don't think they've been picked up by the police. Try and find them.'" Marcus and his comrades would help guide these kids across the South African border. It was dangerous work and had Marcus been caught he would have been thrown in prison or worse.

Marcus said the day he heard of Mandela's release after nearly thirty years in prison felt like falling in love:

"You know the day that we heard the announcement that the ANC is going to be unbanned was the greatest day of my life. And when the announcement came it was it was absolutely crazy! Even people who were never interested in politics rejoiced! We all thought, this is the end of bombs and fights and stones and all of those things, never thinking that we'll still have to march to get Mandela free.

And then when he was released, you know his speech at the Grand Parade? That was great! That was absolutely wonderful! It's difficult to describe the way you felt. It's like when a young man is in love and he asks his girl to become his companion and she says yes—that feeling!"

Choose an Action

Any engagement you choose will have two necessary ingredients: you need to decide on what **action** you will take—i.e., how you will make a difference—and you'll choose an **area of interest**. While there's a good chance you'll choose the action and the issue together—for example, you may learn about a volunteer gig that feels like a good fit—it is helpful at this stage to reflect on them separately so you can get a feel for what actions and issues most draw you.

There's no limit to the ways we can engage. Chapter Five, "Connect," highlights some of the more common vehicles for engagement:

> Join a group
> Volunteer
> Work
> Do your own thing
> Engage politically
> Engage online
> Engage your ethics
> Train to engage
> Drop everything else and engage completely

As you think about possible actions you also might consider:

How you like to spend your time. I find it helpful to recognize that the actions we take as caretakers and changemakers for the most part break down into simple everyday activities: sending emails, showing up for meetings, helping out at events, being there when people need us. If you like working with computers, lots of organizations will happily absorb your skills with websites, databases, and graphics programs. If you're more artistic you can make banners for protests, help paint a mural at the community center, tutor kids in music after school.

Where you want to be. We make a difference in all kinds of spaces: our homes, our schools, our workplaces, in community spaces, on our computers, and in nature. If you like being outdoors, you may want to volunteer at the community garden, clear beaches of plastic, or knock on doors for your political candidate.

How involved do you want to be? A few hours a month, or something more? This new project may require that you let go of existing commitments in order to make time for the new one. And if the project is on a larger scale–perhaps involving a shift in your work life or a move overseas–then your focus will be on the initial steps in what could be a long planning process.

As you consider actions, remember that everyone has different capacities and skills. You may want to undertake something that you don't yet know how to do, or that you may never have the skills to do. You can probably discern the difference.

And, you may be thrown into the deep end like Gwenn Craig, who knew nothing about media relations when Harvey Milk assigned her the role of media coordinator for his political campaign. As Gwenn recalled, "Harvey always had you roped into more than you were originally planning to do. When I first went to Harvey, I went there because I'd gone to this meeting about what was happening in Dade County with Anita Bryant and everything. And I stupidly mouthed off, saying, "We need a very impressive media campaign. I think it's going to really matter what we do with the media. That, I think, is the most important thing." And they said, great, so why don't you do that? So I left there as the media coordinator and I went home and thought, "What the hell did I do?"

EXERCISE: Get a feel for what you might like to do.

Activities I would enjoy doing:_____

Places where I'd like to engage:_____

Time I can put into this: _____

Choose an Area of Focus

Sue King became an environmental educator after realizing how "miserable" she was at the ad agency where she worked in San Francisco. She remembers the day she made the decision to leave: "It was Ash Wednesday and I went to go get my ashes at lunch, and I was in the church and I started crying and I thought 'Oh my God! I've got to get out of here!' I realized I couldn't look for a new job in the state I was in because I was going to end up getting something similar–marketing, PR, some form of sales–and I didn't want to do that. I didn't know where to start."

Sue quit her job, did a series of odd jobs to pay the rent, and took time to reflect on what might be possible. "In all the jobs I'd done, the most satisfying thing was when I was able to work with people and help make a difference. I found where I was at my best was when I would go out of my way to help someone figure something out, or be a problem solver. That was the work that I loved. I thought nonprofits sounded like a pretty good way to do that all the time."

Having decided on nonprofit work, Sue realized there were a lot of different issues that she cared about. "Did I want to work with women, with immigrant populations, with the homeless? It was like, whoa, there were so many things I could do!" She eventually narrowed it down to the environment. "I grew up in a suburban area in New Jersey, close to a huge city where going out and being in nature was always a great solace for me. I was so grateful to have that. I wanted to give other people that opportunity."

Often the issues choose us. Issues that most attract us tend to have some connection to our own lives. Climate change affects everyone. In a recent workshop I offered on bringing mindfulness to action on climate change, eight participants shared almost as many different perspectives on where best to put their energies. Some were more concerned with species extinction, others with carbon emissions legislation, one woman felt passionately about promoting veganism, and others focused more on their personal carbon footprints. Those who were newer to political engagement were more prone to the personal footprint approach; the woman whose focus was on the impacts of diet had been an advocate for veganism for years. Each person's focus reflected their particular experience, knowledge, and background.

In choosing an issue to focus on it can also help to think about what or who you want to support. This could be organizations or individuals or people in a community. Are there groups you give money to that you could imagine joining forces with? What do you feel most passionate about? Which communities do you want to work with? Youth, the elderly, immigrants, prisoners ...? Keep these kinds of questions in mind as you explore.

In an oft-told parable a grandfather tells his granddaughter there are two animals fighting inside his belly, a hungry, angry wolf and a sweet natured dog. Concerned for him, his granddaughter asks, "Which animal wins?" Her grandfather replies, "Whichever one I feed."

The wolf parable cautions us to feed and nurture our own best natures, but it is also a reminder that we get to choose where to put our energies. What do *you* want to help nurture, heal, and grow in the world? This can be your engagement issue.

> **EXERCISE: Refer to the list of issue keywords at the end of the book and circle or note those issues that are most alive and important for you today.** Make a list of the ones that stand out most. If there are too many, then choose the top five or ten.

You May Want to Save the World

Alicia Garza logged into Facebook the day after a jury acquitted George Zimmerman of killing Trayvon Martin. As *Yes! Magazine's* Liz Pleasant reported, Garza "was bombarded with defeatist comments like 'What did you expect?' or 'I knew they would never convict him.' Overwhelmingly, these comments all pointed out the same thing: it's treated as acceptable for unarmed black boys and men to be killed without consequence."

Garza and her friends decided to do something. Garza told *Yes! Magazine* they wanted "a space that people could relate to that didn't blame black people for conditions we didn't create." And so was birthed Black Lives Matter.

Many of us really mean it when we say we want to "save the world." Racism, capitalism, climate change, poverty, population growth, resource depletion, violence, social injustice, economic uncertainty, political corruption: the big, messy, systemic interdependent "issues" are the ones that matter most, which is why we want to take them on. But how can we possibly approach them? **How do we go from wanting to save the world to starting an engagement project?**

When we focus on big and, by their nature, overwhelming issues, we are forced to reflect on what's possible and what's not:

- We need to acknowledge that the desire to respond to the big needs of the world is true and relevant and may require some courage and tenacity on our parts.
- We need to understand that while there's only so much we can do, we *can* do something.
- We need to learn from history. How did people confront big issues like this in the past? What worked? What didn't?
- We need to let go of results.
- We need to be practical about what we personally can do.

What You Can Do

This last point is especially important as you start to define your engagement project. If you want to work on a big "saving the world" kind of project, you'll likely need to do two things: 1) narrow the focus and 2) join with others who are engaging the same topic.

> **Narrow the focus.** Get specific. I learned this from Miki Kashtan, who was the social change coordinator for the Center for Nonviolent Communication in 2003. I asked her how to work with feeling anger over a big issue like capitalism and wanting to do something about it. Miki suggested: "As long as you don't have an actual observation of who is doing what that

you are angry at that you want to see changed, it will be vague and diffuse and it will not lead to concrete action in the world. What does capitalism mean to you? Which part of capitalism are you angry about? 'Oh, well I'm angry at the whole thing.' *Pick a piece that particularly stands out to you.* Maybe it leads you to the International Monetary Fund because of the pressure they put on countries to accept structural adjustment in order to receive loans. That's the place where you want to put your energy."

Join with others. Find out who is already confronting the big issue you care about, that you might want to join and work with. Studs Terkel wrote in *Hope Dies Last* that to confront our greatest common challenges we need, "a legion of Davids, with all sorts of slingshots. It's not one slingshot that will do it. Nor will it happen at once. It's a long haul."

One of my favorite "slingshot" stories is the unlikely coalition that formed between farmers, landowners, school teachers, Republicans, Democrats, cowboys, and Indians in opposition to the Keystone XL pipeline in Nebraska. Building from small groups getting together in kitchens and community halls, this alliance of Davids tripped up the Goliath of Big Oil and dirty politics that dominates the Nebraska legislature, and actually helped halt the passage of the dirtiest oil in the world through their state.

And how did they do it? They talked to each other about their concerns for their land, their wildlife, and the future of their children and grandchildren. They built popular support. As author Mary Pipher tells us in *The Green Boat*, they didn't give up:

"As our group learned to discuss weighty matters with each other and still be calm and hopeful, we developed ideas for how to approach other people. In fact, our most common topic was communication. We quickly realized that what we knew was only useful if we could say it in ways that encouraged other people to listen and act. … We mostly talked about what we were for, not what we were against. With almost everyone, we could find common ground and stay there. Who doesn't like clean water, green pastures, and healthy animals?"

It is through our little engagement projects that we save the world; saving the world and engagement projects have everything to do with one another.

> **EXERCISE: Write some ideas down about what you might do for an engagement project.** Keep it simple. You're just trying these on.

Whatever You Do, Enjoy It

As you complete this chapter I hope some ideas have surfaced about what kind of engagement project you might do. There is no need to make a decision, yet. The point of this chapter was to stir up some ideas.

Once you decide on an engagement project I hope you will do something you like. It's fine, of course, to stretch your skills and learning and even your comfort zone. When we engage in something new we can wind up in unexpected and unfamiliar situations. But beware of undertaking a project out of a sense of guilt or "I should." Choose something that really interests you and, if possible, that you feel passionate about.

My first memory of engaging was when I was in high school during the East African famine in the 1980s. We were all horrified seeing images of people starving on TV. My friend Laurie and I talked about what we might do, and we and other members of the after school club called the Socially Enabling Enacting Society, decided to hold a fundraiser. We raised $237 dollars at our school, which we hand-delivered to the aid agency's warehouse in San Francisco. When we got there, volunteers were sorting through bags of donated food and clothing, preparing these to be loaded on a freighter to East Africa. It was exciting to see up close the impact of our small donation. It felt good to bring them the money, and the people we gave it to were very grateful. What we did was small, but at the same time it felt so right.

In contrast, also in high school, I volunteered at a home for the elderly as part a class requirement. I did not connect in any memorable way with the people we visited. What I remember about those visits was feeling uncomfortable and directionless and unclear about what to do.

These were two very different experiences. One was empowering. I learned from it, I was motivated, interested, and I cared. The other was depressing and made me feel somewhat inadequate. I didn't really want to be there (but I thought I *should* want to be there). I put my heart into the fundraising, but not into the visits with the elderly.

As my friend Jon put it, "If people get involved in things that they're attracted to–rather than out of a sense of obligation–they're more likely to do good work."

> **EXERCISE: This engagement project is about you.** In what way do you hope that doing an engagement project will make your own life better? Consider if it would benefit you to make a list of criteria for your engagement project, including emotional needs, types of activities, specific people, locations, and/or existing groups you could join.

EXPLORING EXERCISES

1. **Describe ways you have engaged in caretaking or changemaking in the past or present, if this applies to you**. Break it down into the nitty-gritty kinds of tasks you've done as part of that engagement. What does making a difference look and feel like? How did/do you spend your time? Reflect on whether these are the kinds of tasks you'd like to do as part of your engagement project.

2. **Friends who engage**. Are there people in your life who engage in ways you admire or that interest you? What do they do? What kind of impact do you think they have? Are they doing things you'd like to be doing? Are they people you would want to work with?

3. **What do you enjoy (and not) doing at work?** What do you enjoy most in work situations? What do you wish you could do more of? What could you do without? What would you like never to have to do again? Make some lists and consider how this can help you think about future engagement activities.

4. **Connect.** List all the organizations and people you think you would want to work (or volunteer or take action) with. Reflect on why these groups and people. Even if you plan to "do your own thing," make this list so you can think about who out there you may end up connecting with around your interests.

5. **Helping others.** Spend a few minutes writing about a time when you have helped someone in need. It could be a friend going through a difficult time emotionally or a relative who broke a leg or an older relative who needed a lift. How did it feel to support them? How did they receive your support?

6. **What kinds of actions appeal to you?** Which activities below are you drawn to and which not? What would you add to the list? Reflect on both what does and does not interest you and why.

   - Volunteer in a health clinic, social service agency, mental health clinic, etc.
   - Work or volunteer for a human rights, social justice, or environmental action group.
   - Help put on an informational community event.

- Work as part of a renewable energy enterprise.
- Fundraise for victims of natural disasters.
- Tutor young children one-on-one.
- Participate in a study group to learn about a specific current issue.
- Participate in nonviolent direct action.

7. **Engage your power.** This is a detailed exercise but well worth the time. It's my favorite exercise in the book. Allow 15-30 minutes to do this one.

- Write down one change you want to see take place in the world. This could be a shift in government policy on a particular issue, a new health clinic in your town, moving animals off of endangered species lists, inspiring others to act, etc. Anything, any size.
- Write down any one thing *you know you personally can do* to help bring about that change.
- Write down one thing *you know you cannot do* to bring about that change (something necessary for the change to take place).
- What *external* circumstances (e.g., organizations, people, systems) are likely to limit your ability to act?
- What *internal* limitations (e.g., personal habits, economic resources, knowledge) might prevent you from helping bring about this change?
- What circumstances would make it possible for you to make this change happen? Use your imagination. Would you need political or economic power, the support of particular people, money or land or other resources, technical ability or expertise?
- Does any single group or person in the world have the power to make this change?
- How might you work with this group or person?

Alberto: *If an activist is honest with you, the burnout is a recurring phenomenon and you learn how to cope with it or you just never keep it up. It's impossible to be an activist and not get burned out. Impossible.*

Interview with Alberto Saldamando in San Francisco, California in 1999, on "Political Engagement."

Kerry: *What is it that causes people to censor themselves?*

Louise: *Fear, fear, and fear! When I realized I had to write a whole chapter on this for my book, I had a lot of fun thinking about what are all the factors in it. People don't have self-esteem. Everything they've encountered in society—their parents, their schooling, their teachers, their workplace—the whole culture has reinforced this feeling that you're nothing. You're a cog in the wheel. Children should be seen and not heard. It's dangerous to speak out. A few years ago a Veterans Administration nurse spoke out about the suicide rate of returning veterans from Iraq and was very critical of the army policy about that. She lost her job. But this happens everywhere. Each person has a different story of silencing.*

Joanna: *And that's embedded by the isolation in which we live. This is a nation of lonely and isolated people. It is a competitive, industrialized, consumer culture. You don't feel you have the support of others in speaking out.*

Louise: *Yes. And you don't feel heard. You can't speak out if you know people aren't listening to you or are discounting or marginalizing you. It just doesn't come out right.*

Joanna: *I think it's fear of pain—of moral pain. Of feeling the suffering of our world.*

Louise: *One man said that in a workshop I gave in New Orleans about six months after Katrina. We were discussing "what makes us silent." And he said "I don't want to write these things that I've just learned about our government because I fear that if I really say the truth that it will be too awful even for me to bear. The truth is too awful. It will hurt me."*

Interview with Joanna Macy and Louise Dunlap in Berkeley, California, in 2010, on "Facilitating Social Change."

WEEK FOUR: UNBLOCK

Notice what's stopping you

"We have a saying in Tibet that engaging in the practice of virtue is as hard as driving a donkey uphill, whereas engaging in destructive activities is as easy as rolling boulders downhill."

–The Dalai Lama

Years ago a giant boulder rolled down a hill and landed in the center of a busy canyon road in Los Angeles. The boulder was as tall as a telephone pole, and blocked traffic completely going both directions.

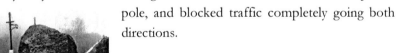

They left it there. For years no one could drive down that road. Just kidding. Of course the city found a way to break apart and remove the boulder so the traffic could flow once again.

Last week you explored what you might do. This week is about the stop signs and detours that are an inevitable part of engaging.

A "block" refers to any situation or experience of wanting to move forward and being unable to. As aspiring engagers the kinds of blocks we meet may include: internal, external, monetary, time, skills, organizational, logistical, emotional, body issues, mind issues, apathy, anger, worry, fear, overwhelm, sadness, guilt, self-judgment, political, cultural, confidence, procrastination, imaginary, creative, ecological, spiritual, past experiences, historical, big, small, likes, dislikes, long-term, short-term, communication, difficult people, interpersonal, motivational, insurmountable, healthy boundaries, ideological, family expectations…

We all experience blocks to engaging. They are usually temporary, sometimes helpful (corrective or protective), often a necessary stage in a learning or healing process. Once we get past one issue, we will likely encounter more on the path ahead. "Turning back is how the Way moves," said Lao Tzu. And Rumi reminds us, "Your hand opens and closes and opens and closes. If it were always a fist or always stretched open, you would be paralyzed."

A block is like the guard at the palace gate challenging, "Who goes there?!" And, "Why should I let *you* in?" Blocks test our patience, certainty, and tenacity on the quest to making a difference.

Blocks to Engaging

The first and often biggest hurdle to making a difference is making the initial decision to do something. I've long wondered what it is that makes this first step so difficult for people. Years ago in an effort to better understand what keeps people from engaging, I circulated a casual survey to friends, offering the following list of multiple-choice possibilities:

- Too many other commitments or priorities
- Not enough time
- Procrastination
- Not liking the culture of activists/activism
- I feel anxious when I think about engaging
- Overwhelmed by all the problems
- Uncertain that my actions will make a difference

Most of the fifty people who responded said they were blocked by "too many other commitments or priorities" and "not enough time." Many were also put off by the "culture of activists/activism." When asked "What could help you engage?" about half agreed with the statement "faith that my actions would bear fruit."

What struck me most about the survey was how very involved those who responded already were. In the prior three years most had volunteered, signed online petitions, donated money, and done something to "Green" their lives. Many had jobs in the nonprofit and service sectors. A few were activists. And yet they still felt stuck. They wanted to do more, but, as some shared in comments:

"I'm not sure I have much to offer."

"I don't know how to find the right group to join."

"I'm preoccupied with making a living."

"Overall, I find it hard to remain engaged when bombarded with bad news, and I find myself skeptical that the current methods of activism work."

Meeting the Block

 Once we decide to engage, the blocks we come across are often an unpleasant surprise. There's a boulder on the road! What's that doing there?!

Hurdles we can encounter at this stage include:

Indecision about what project to do.

Wondering if we have the skills required.

Worry about how much time we can commit.

Procrastination.

Once the engagement project gets off the ground we encounter new ones:

We join a group that doesn't jell and start skipping meetings.

We join a letter writing campaign and experience writer's block.

We've been matched up to tutor someone we don't have a good rapport with.

We aren't confident we can do the task we've signed up for.

Some of our obstructions look familiar. That's because we know them well. "I hate it when people act like that." Or, "I wish I was more capable." Or, "It's hard taking this on when I have so many other commitments." Or, "I can't write." And encountering the difficulties we can lose our enthusiasm and momentum and just stop showing up.

As soon as we encounter a block, there's a decision to be made. Do we keep trying to move forward or is it better to turn back? Is it worth trying to make this work?

This is where it gets interesting, because as we look more closely at the situation there's often something to learn. Blocks have layers; slice into one, and you may find that your uncertainty about transitioning from for-profit to work in the nonprofit sector is not entirely about making less money, but also because you're not convinced that the job will be an effective avenue for creating change. Emotional issues may surface as you grapple with practical problems: sadness and overwhelm related to world issues, guilt for not having done something sooner, or wishing you were more courageous.

Working with Blocks

Blocks to taking action don't stop us forever. Shiloh Barnat, a long-time activist, wanted to protest the U.S. bombing of Iraq in 2002. But she had recently moved from San Francisco to Memphis and no one seemed to be protesting. She said, "I felt incredibly depressed and saddened and furious. I wanted to do something. But that wasn't happening here. And I didn't know where to reach out."

Shiloh eventually found a progressive community in Memphis with the Quakers and a local Peace and Justice Center. It just took time. She learned from the initial frustration of not knowing anyone how essential being part of a community was for her activism. "It's much easier and safer to do something that you care about if you're with other people who are also doing that. When I don't feel connected to the people around me I am less likely to do anything about the issues that I care about."

There are many ways to work with blocks.

Patience is often the key. Very often what is blocked is the desire to take action right now. "I want everything to happen immediately," my friend Pramod said at a time when he was looking into starting a bio-diesel business. "I'm forming alliances with people who are interested and trying to whip up enthusiasm. The pace is extremely slow, but it's starting to happen."

Prioritizing our engagement work over other interests can help. If it isn't a priority, then you are more likely to give up. If you're determined to see it through, you will likely find a way. My friend Elizabeth tied herself to her chair to help herself stick with the long and daunting task of writing her dissertation.

Affirming why our engagement work matters can help motivate us. Turn back to what motivates you from your work in Week Two; those positive intentions are energizing and inspiring and always a source for us to tap when we feel discouraged.

Finally, try to **be kind to yourself as you encounter blocks**. We want to encourage ourselves to work with the blocks, not force ourselves. Being blocked isn't easy, and we don't want to make it harder by guilt tripping, criticizing, or blaming ourselves for the problems that arise.

The remainder of this chapter offers a review of some specific blocks we encounter and suggests possible approaches for working with them. Sometimes I suggest you greet the block creatively, and other times I suggest you stop trying to make what really is a block "work." Blocks both hinder us and protect us, and it's important to understand the distinction.

> **EXERCISE: In what ways do you feel blocked around
> engaging?** Write about your experience. Write too about what
> might help you move things along.

Time

Issues

- I'm too busy to start something new right now.
- Getting involved will take up too much of my free time.
- No matter how much time I devote to the project it will never be enough, so why bother?
- I'm unclear about how much I'm willing to give right now.

Possible Approaches

- Drop an activity in exchange for this new one.
- Consider what you might do to free up time. For example, if you have kids, could you get child care? Could other family members or friends help out?
- Try committing a very small amount of time each day/week/month to your activity. Can you spend an hour a week doing this? Half an hour? Sometimes even the smallest commitment can bear fruit.

- Do you see engaging as a burden or as a drain on your energy? If so, make a list of ways engaging now would be burdensome and in what ways energizing.
- Keep in mind that like physical exercise, the time we spend in our engagement is good for us. It's about our needs. It's heart time. For example, studies show that people who volunteer are less prone to heart disease. We need to exercise this muscle.

Disorganization

Issues

- I can't seem to get organized.
- I have too many good ideas and can't decide which one to do.
- I need a plan in place before I can engage.

Possible Approaches

- Work with planning tools, starting with some that are in this book.
- Reflect on whether planning as an obstacle is really about procrastination. If so, you might try free writing on why and how you are procrastinating (hopefully without falling into self-judgment).
- Don't try to get organized. Read up on different issues and activities that attract you. Take the pressure off yourself to "produce" or get started just yet. You obviously want to do something, but you may not actually have the time or "space" to take it on yet.

I Don't Know What to Do

Issues

- I want to save the whole world.
- I want to work on everything at once.
- I have no idea where to focus.

Possible Approaches

- Realize it's OK that you don't know exactly what you want to do. Rather than trying to figure it out or force an answer, start by reflecting on why you are interested in engaging.
- Remember that whatever you choose to do you will be making one small difference along with others who are also contributing. No one can save the world, but we each get to contribute a little.
- Use creative tools. Try making a collage of issues you care about–using cuttings from magazines, for example. Or try drawing, painting, free-form writing. You may notice some issues are emerging more strongly than others, or that what you are drawn to cut out of the magazines has a particular focus.
- Try this drawing exercise. Draw your home and a stick figure of you at your home. Then draw a road and imagine yourself walking on that road towards the place you will engage. See if anything emerges–a destination that shows where you would feel "right" as a place of engagement. It may be a physical place, an organization, or images of specific people. You may even see yourself in a role. But start with where you are now and walk the image of yourself towards that place.
- Notice what issues most interest you. When you talk with friends and family about the news, what issues or concerns do you tend to bring up a lot? If you keep saying something over and over it may be that is where you need start working.
- Do you know people (preferably friends or acquaintances you like) who are engaged in something you could see yourself engaged in? This could be a good starting place.
- Take your time.

I Don't Like Activists

Issues

- I don't like activists.
- I don't identify as an activist.
- I don't like the culture of activism.

Possible Approaches

- Forget the term. Instead break it down. What is attracting you to the kind of work that "activists" do?
- What goals do you share with activists?
- What groups would you join if you weren't put off by activism?
- What forms of activism are OK with you?
- Redefine "activism" so that it includes you and what you want to do. Were Nelson Mandela, Martin Luther King, and Gandhi activists? Are Malala Yousafzai and Edward Snowden? And if they are not activists, what do we call them and their supporters?

I Don't Like Politics

Issues

- I distrust politicians.
- I think the political system is corrupt so why work with it?
- I question my (or anyone's) ability to have an impact through the political system.

Possible Approaches

- As with the block of not liking activism, you may feel pulled in two directions—on the one hand recognizing that the government is powerful, while on the other that politicians are beholden to special interests and therefore not to be trusted (or something along those lines).
- Reflect on both the positives and negatives of political involvement.
- Consider why you would want to be a politician or why you might want to support a candidate or get involved in party politics. What can politicians achieve?
- Are there any politicians you believe are doing a good job despite the system?
- Consider the strengths and weaknesses of working at different levels of government—local, state, federal. If you were to engage politically where might you be most effective?

Disconnection

"I know I am not alone. There must be hundreds of other women, maybe thousands, who feel as I do. But how do you hook up with them? How can you interlink your own struggle and goals with these myriad hypothetical people?"
—June Jordan

Issues

- I don't know who to talk to about this issue.
- I don't know anyone who understands or shares my concerns.

Possible Approaches

- Start sharing your interest in engaging with friends, co-workers, classmates, family. Ask their advice. See what they have to share. Maybe they know people you can connect with.
- Research what organizations in your area are working on the concerns that interest you.
- Write about the ways your life intersects with the issues you are thinking of engaging.
- Write about and reflect on why these issues are so important to you.

Emotional Blocks

"To be separate means to be helpless, unable to grasp the world—things and people—actively; it means that the world can invade me without my ability to react."
—Erich Fromm

"You can't control how you feel," Buddhist teacher Sally Armstrong said once on a meditation retreat. In our dramas about what stops our engagement, emotions play the lead roles. Emotions that stop us from acting include fear, confusion, anger, discouragement, and heartbreak. Ironically, these same emotions can ultimately move us to act as well.

When we do this kind of work, some of our emotions will be motivating, while others can stop us in our tracks. Can we learn to feel the difficult emotions and still be active? What can we do when we get stuck?

Here are some emotions you may recognize that relate to engaging in service or action:

caring	fear	righteousness
concern	despair	excitement
compassion	inspiration	frustration
numbness	disappointment	urgency
anger	determination	overwhelm
outrage	hope	

Psychologist John Amodeo says, "Giving our feelings space gives them room to breathe and move, rather than staying stuck. Oftentimes we're not gentle toward our feelings. We may think something is wrong with us for having feelings such as fear, sadness, or shame. We may try to push these parts of ourselves away in a misguided attempt to feel better or look good."

And Joanna Macy reminds us, "They're just feelings. They come and go, and we're only stuck with what we're resisting, what we're trying to hold at arm's length–that's when we're stuck. But if we speak the fear, speak the grief, speak the outrage, and the emptiness then you're free from it in a very real way."

EXERCISE: How are you feeling? Take a few minutes to write about what emotions come up for you around the issues you are planning to engage. Also, how are you feeling about the prospect of starting your engagement project?

Apathy and Hopelessness

"Probably the most frequent response to the mention of any global threat is to the effect that 'I don't think about that because there is nothing I can do about it.' Logically, this is a non sequitur, confusing what can be thought and felt with what can be done."

–Joanna Macy and Molly Young Brown

Issues

- It doesn't matter if I do anything.
- I don't have any energy.
- What's the point?
- I feel depressed about the state of the world.

Possible Approaches

- Why did you pick up this book? Write about why you feel like you want to do something, even if you believe it won't have an impact. Write about why you think you want to be active.
- Make two lists: all the things that give you energy and all the things that drain your energy. Use your lists. The next time you feel apathetic, turn to the list of things that give you energy and try doing a couple of them and see if your mood or view shifts.
- Write about why it is OK not to do anything right now. Why does it make sense that you feel apathetic or overwhelmed about the state of the world? Or depressed?
- Write about what a screwed-up place the world is right now.
- Know that it's OK to feel apathetic or hopeless about the state of the world and your contribution to it. You can see this apathy and just let it be. You don't need to try to change the feeling. It's an honest response to the state of the world. You'll become active when you're ready.

In *The Green Boat* Mary Pipher tells about a study on people's responses to climate change. The study "found that people actually care intensely about the environment, but that their emotions are tangled up and upsetting and they are so beset by internal conflicts that they cannot act adaptively. They are not apathetic, but rather in psychological shutdown."

Overwhelm and Burnout

"To allow ourselves to be carried away by a multitude of conflicting concerns, to surrender to too many demands, to commit oneself to too many projects, to want to help everyone and everything is to succumb to violence."

–Thomas Merton

Issues

- It's too much.
- There are too many causes that need my attention.
- I'm overwhelmed by all the information.
- There are too many directions to choose from.
- I can't do this anymore.

Possible Approaches

- Take one small step at a time. You're reading this book because you want to do something. Is there some small (even miniscule) action you feel you can do that won't overwhelm you or stress you out?
- Remember we're all in this together. It's not all on your shoulders. Consider talking with others who share your concerns and who may also be feeling overwhelmed. Appreciate we are each doing our best.
- Take a break. Come back later. Really, it's OK not to be active. You may need to rest for a while. Have compassion for your desire to do something at a time when you may not have the energy or heart to engage.

- If you're feeling burned out, you might try focusing elsewhere. Longtime activist Alberto Saldamando copes with burnout by moving on to other interests after a time. He said in an interview, "I've always coped with burnout by looking for something else to do. Something that interests you, that's different. It can't be less stressful, 'cause I think activism per se is stressful. It makes big demands on your personal life. It makes big demands on your time."
- If you're overwhelmed by the magnitude of a problem, take a look at Miki's suggestion in Week Three and see if you can narrow your focus and get more specific about ways to contribute.

Sadness and Despair

"The single mood people generally put the most effort into shaking is sadness."
–Daniel Goldman

"When we deny or repress our pain for the world, or treat it as a private pathology, our power to take part in the healing of our world is diminished."
–Joanna Macy

Issues

- I don't follow the news about this issue because it makes me too sad.
- I feel heartbroken about the issues we are confronting.
- How can people treat each other and the earth this way? What's wrong with us?
- It's hopeless.
- It's too painful to face.

Possible Approaches

- Hang out with the sadness when it comes up. You may need to cry or in some way express what you are feeling. You might take a walk with this sadness, or talk with a friend. Give the sadness space to be felt and seen.
- Know that your sadness makes perfect sense. It makes sense that you can't take this one in, or be as present as you might want to be. Know that in time the situation will change and that most likely healing, or at least ease will be possible.
- Take a few minutes to reflect on or freewrite about any situation that you usually experience as too awful to bring your focus to. See and feel how bad it is. Remember you are not alone in your caring and concern for the person or people harmed by this painful situation. Remember that what you are feeling, others are feeling.
- Do you, or can you, feel compassion for those harmed in this situation? Compassion feels like the blanket we wrap around those we love when they need some comfort. We want to envelop those in need in love and warmth. Robert Cusick who trains people in developing compassion says, "When the pain we experience manifests as compassion we let go of the conflict of the pain. Compassion acknowledges the suffering without being lost in it."
- See if you can have compassion for yourself as you face this situation.

Worry

Issues

- I worry a lot about what is happening in the world.
- I feel anxious and depressed about world events.
- I feel anxious when I think about getting involved.
- I'm too stressed out to make rational decisions about what to do next.

Possible Approaches

- Recognize there are reasons it may make sense for you to worry and see if you can have compassion for yourself and others who are also stressed out about the world and how to engage.
- Remember you're not alone in your concern or in your worrying behavior.
- Write down all your worries on a piece of paper. Take a look at what you've written. Make a paper airplane with this list, or burn it. Let those worries go.
- Write a letter to the President, or your god, or mother earth expressing all your concerns about the country/world. Maybe even send the letter.
- Make a small donation to a group involved in one of the issues you are anxious about.
- If you think you should be involved in a particular issue but your heart isn't in it, don't force it. In time you may be stirred to action. See what happens if you let go for a while.
- Consider signing up for a Mindfulness Based Stress Reduction class.

Worry and anxiety have the mystifying ability to make us feel as if we are actually doing something when we are not. When I worry about saving the world it gives me a feeling that I am engaged in saving the world because that is where my attention is. But of course I'm just worried.

We need to be able to express our worry and anxiety so it can move through us and we can move on. Worries need to be released. This is why simple activities like writing letters can help. Consider other ways you can release rather than be caught in the hamster wheel of your overly anxious mind.

Anger

Issues

- I'm so mad I can't think straight.
- I'm outraged.

- I feel deeply frustrated because no one is adequately addressing this issue.
- I don't engage because I don't want to be upset.
- I'm upset by anger in people I engage with.

Possible Approaches

- Breathe.
- Don't deny the anger or try to bypass it. Can you accept that you are angry?
- Talk to friends about the anger.
- Vent: punch pillows, stomp around on the ground, take a long hike, go to the gym or a kickboxing class.
- Take care of the anger without relating to it as "your" anger. Be understanding of the anger. Listen to the anger as it were a good friend.
- Do the nonviolent communication exercise that peace activist Mike Adams suggests in the next chapter: First throw a temper tantrum on paper, and then write the letter to the corporation that is polluting the river you care about in such a way that the "polluters" can listen.
- Read Thich Nhat Hanh's book *Anger: Wisdom for Cooling the Flames.*

I used to drive in Bay Area traffic in a state of utter frustration. A trip across the Bay Bridge that should have taken twenty minutes would take an hour. I'd be inching forward in an old car (no air-conditioning), anxious to get to an exit. One day I realized that part of my frustration lay in the fact that I kept noticing the obstructions in the traffic–the brakes to my progress–rather than the openings. And I realized that when I focused on not moving I was frustrated. When I focused on the movement and the gaps between the cars then I drove with more ease. When I was able to reframe my experience my anger and anxiety diminished.

Self-Judgment and Guilt

"Convinced that we are not good enough, we can never relax. We stay on guard, monitoring ourselves for shortcomings. When we inevitably find them, we feel even more insecure and undeserving."

–Tara Brach

Issues

- Anyone would do this better than me.
- I feel guilty that it has taken me so long to get involved.
- I've failed in the past and I'm sure I'll fail again if I try.
- I'm not smart enough, disciplined enough, talented enough, etc.

Possible Approaches

- Do the "inner critic" exercise at the end of this chapter.
- Recognize that the negative voice doesn't serve you or your cause.
- Reflect on whether anything positive is coming out of your judgments about your lack of abilities. If you can't think of anything positive consider whether it makes sense to listen to this voice. If you can think of a positive–such as you may not be ready for this particular engagement–then reflect on whether the judging voice is in some way protecting you.
- Read Byron Brown's *Soul without Shame* or Tara Brach's *Radical Acceptance: Embracing Your Life with the Heart of a Buddha* and really examine how shame and judgment operate in your life.
- Turn to tools for self-compassion. Kristin Neff's book *Self Compassion: The Proven Power of Being Kind to Yourself* is a good one. Neff writes: "Self-compassion provides an island of calm, a refuge from the stormy seas of endless positive and negative self-judgement so that we can finally stop asking, 'Am I as good as they are? Am I good enough?' By tapping into our wellsprings of kindness, acknowledging the shared nature of our imperfect human condition, we can start to feel more secure, accepted and alive."

UNBLOCKING EXERCISES

1. **What emotional blocks do you encounter and how might you work with them?**

2. **What logistical blocks stop you from taking action and how can you work with them?**

3. **How have you experienced blocks in the past?** Describe any situation in which you have felt blocked around doing something that was important to you. What did you do when this happened? How did the issue/blockage resolve? Is there any advice you wish you could give your younger self who was blocked?

4. **What can help you work with your blocks?** Write a paragraph or more about working with, around, or through blocks to engaging.

5. **Notice when you go numb.** Numbing out is different from relaxing, although we can easily confuse the two. In what circumstances do you find yourself tuning out? Try noticing if when you turn on the smartphone or computer, you do so to avoid feeling something happening in that moment. Are there some activities you do to relax that seem more "healthy" than others? What ways of relaxing are nurturing for you?

6. **Notice your inner critic.** Inner judges and critics are a mixed bag. They can guide us in our choices but they can also be stern, cold, and without empathy as they scrutinize our work, our life. Fairy godmothers are spirits of support, gentleness, caring. We carry both of these archetypal voices within us. Write for five to ten minutes on both your judge and your fairy godmother as follows:

   a. First, describe your internal judge or critic as a person or character: What do they look like? How do they act? What do they tell you about your desire to contribute? How do you react to the voice of the judge?

   b. Next, describe your inner fairy godmother. Same thing: How does she look and act? What words does she offer in relationship to the work you what to do? What does she appreciate about you? How do you feel when she's present?

7. **Engagement project check-in**. Next week you'll choose your engagement project. How are you doing with this exploration? Has the work you've done this week impacted the direction of your project at all?

ENTERING ENGAGEMENT

Kerry: *Can you change the world?*

Gwenn: *In very small incremental ways, definitely. I went to the 1980 Democratic National Convention. I sat there in my seat and I had a big sign that I'd made that said "Black Lesbian Feminist." And I held it up every time there was applause or something. And all these cameras would come. It was on the front page of the Washington Post. I think that that made a difference.*

Dennis: *I'd say you can change parts of some worlds. You can change your own world, if you're lucky enough. I feel I have made a tremendous difference in hundreds of people's lives! I will say almost anything. I make it easier for other people to talk about themselves and not feel like they're weird. And I know for a lot of people that's really been a good thing. You know we all came out of the closet, but some of us were slower. I brought lots of my friends out. I feel like I've made a difference in my own life and my friends and the people I've helped come out.*

Interview with Dennis Seely and Gwenn Craig in San Francisco, California in 1999,
on "Political Engagement."

WEEK FIVE: CONNECT

Choose your project

"Much of an organizer's daily work is detail, repetitive and deadly in its monotony. In the totality of things he is engaged in one small bit. It is as though as an artist he is painting a tiny leaf. It is inevitable that sooner or later he will react with 'what am I doing spending my whole life just painting one little leaf? The hell with it, I quit.' What keeps him going is a blurred vision of a great mural where other artists—organizers—are painting their bits, and each piece is essential to the total."
–Saul Alinsky

Ways We Engage

This week you begin your engagement project!

You've spent four weeks exploring your interests, motivations, and blocks to engaging, and are now ready to take your first steps. This week and next you will hone and refine your engagement project idea and better acquaint yourself with your field of engagement.

This chapter offers an overview of some of the ways you can engage:

Join or start a group	Engage online
Volunteer	Do your own thing
Work	Engage your ethics
Engage politically	Train to Engage
Write letters	Engage completely

If you are still unsure how you want to engage, this chapter is for you. If you have already decided on an action, you might use this chapter to get a feel for other options and ideas. **Either way, be sure to do the *Exercises* section at the end of the chapter so you can get started on your project.**

Join or Start a Group

"Over the last 40 years, Greenpeace has helped to end nuclear testing, introduce a ban on the dumping of radioactive waste at sea, protect the ozone layer by introducing technology like 'Greenfreeze' refrigeration, establish a treaty to protect the Antarctic from mineral exploration, and put an end to commercial whale hunting."
–Kumi Naidoo

Although you *can* act alone to make an impact on the world, most people end up working within groups or organizations. There are all kinds of groups: schools, nonprofits, affinity groups, political groups, support groups, etc. You can find or start groups at work, at school, within your neighborhood, or within your religious or spiritual community. Groups are also online, and in the streets.

Some good reasons to work in groups:

- **Effectiveness**. With a group of people you have the potential to turn that single letter to the editor into a letter writing campaign.
- **Power**. To quote Margaret Mead, "Never doubt that a small group of thoughtful, committed citizens can change the world. Indeed, it is the only thing that ever has."
- **Support**. It feels emotionally supportive to be in a room full of like-minded people who want to take on a shared cause or concern.
- **Energy and Creativity**. In groups we energize each other and spur one another's creativity.
- **Making space**. When you're part of a group you help to create a place for others to join in and become active or offer service.

Rosa Parks was a member of the Student Nonviolent Coordinating Committee (SNCC) when she chose to sit in the front of the bus; Nelson Mandela was a member of the African National Congress (ANC) for six decades. Each has become larger than life, and it's easy to admire their heroism, but it's important to remember that each took action representing their organizations, as well as the greater communities and causes their organizations advocated for.

How to Find a Group

Go online. Do keyword searches for your focus area and your location.

Search websites like craigslist.org and meetup.com to see if there are local groups listed.

Go to your local library, college, or community center and look for postings, or ask for suggestions from staff.

Contact an organization that campaigns nationally or internationally on your issue, e.g., groups like Amnesty International, American Friends Service Committee, Public Citizen, Human Rights Watch, Idle No More, and Doctors Without Borders.

Look for notices in progressive journals and webzines like *Utne*, *The Nation*, *Z Magazine*, *Yes! Magazine*.

Contact local religious or labor groups. Unions often engage in national campaigns. Place of worship may have committees or group members working on issues that interest you.

Network with friends and see if they have any suggestions.

Join a study group. *The Nation* (www.thenation.org) and *Utne Reader* (www.utne.com) host study groups that meet regularly in various locations in the U.S. Or try the study circle model offered by the Study Circles Resource Center (www.studycircles.org).

How to Start a Group

If you don't want to join an existing group, start your own.

First, contact friends you'd like to work with who share your concern. Set a date for a meeting. If you are willing to work with people you don't know, post fliers in your area to let people know about the meeting or post notices on sites like craigslist.org or meetup.com.

Prepare for your first meeting:

- Designate someone to convene and initially take responsibility for the group.
- Set a clear agenda.
- Set a time limit for the meeting.
- Pass around a contact sheet so you have everyone's name, phone, and email.
- At your first or second meeting establish protocols for speaking and decision-making.
- As the initiator you need to offer a clear vision of what kinds of activities you'd like the group to undertake and articulate any specific goals you would like the group to accomplish.

There's a great range activities your group can undertake: create and distribute educational resources, write letters, go to events together, read and study together, hold vigils, etc.

Volunteer

"Research demonstrates that volunteering leads to better health and that older volunteers are most likely to receive physical and mental health benefits from their volunteer activities."
—Corporation for National and Community Service

In his book *Make a Difference: Your Guide to Volunteering*, Arthur Blaustein tells how one woman was moved by her experience of tutoring kids after school: "Never did I anticipate the emotional attachment that I now share with these children. I find myself yearning to become a teacher, which was a career I never thought about before this program. I know that as these children grow, they will probably forget about me;

but I know I will never forget them. I have truly changed and matured as a result of them."

What do volunteers do? Pretty much everything. I've stuffed envelopes, hung flyers on doorknobs, worked on long-term projects doing research; I even helped to start up a nonprofit. There are many, many different ways to volunteer your time without playing the traditional roles we may associate with the word "volunteer."

Why volunteer? For one thing, your help is needed. Many nonprofits would not survive without volunteer help. Also, volunteering is fun and interesting. It also feels good. "Research suggests that there's an emotional, visceral connection to volunteering that just cannot be duplicated by writing a check," said Brad Hewitt of Minneapolis-based Thrivent Financial for Lutherans, which commissioned a survey on giving.

Some people volunteer as a first step towards working for an organization; it is sometimes a way "in" to a group that may not have many job opportunities. Volunteering is also a good way to gain experience and knowledge about a specific issue.

If you do volunteer, be clear with the group you work for about how much time you can give each week or month. You also need to be clear about what kinds of work you are and are not willing to do. From the point of view of the group you serve, it's also important that you follow through on whatever time commitments you make; when volunteering, it can be easy to shrug off the importance of your work because you are giving your time for free. But not following through can create problems for a group that comes to depend on you.

If you are a high school, college student or recent graduate you may consider doing an **internship**. Interns usually work in exchange for education credits and/or a small stipend. Sometimes you'll write a paper or complete a specific task as part of your internship. If you are a college student, go to the career counseling office at your school to find out about internship opportunities.

How to Find Volunteer Positions

In addition to finding volunteer listings on the websites of specific groups, some sites will help match you up with volunteer opportunities. Here is a small sample of places to start:

- Volunteermatch.org
- Idealist.org
- Guidestar.org

There are also "volunteer centers" in many urban areas that can put you in contact with local groups seeking volunteers. Do a web search on "volunteer center" and your city or county to see if there is one in your area.

Work

"My hope is that whatever you do to make a good life for yourself–whether you become a teacher, or social worker, or business person, or lawyer, or poet, or scientist–you will devote part of your life to making this a better world for your children, for all children." –Howard Zinn, *Spelman College Commencement Address*

Your engagement project could be a job search. It's a rare commencement speech that doesn't implore young graduates to go out and make a difference. And this is very possible. There are plenty of avenues for engaging through work. What can be tricky is finding a livelihood that is meaningful in ways that approximate your specific interests, while also offering you sufficient income and job satisfaction.

Studs Terkel's 1972 classic book, *Working*, begins, "This book, being about work, is, by its very nature, about violence – to the spirit as well as to the body." He continues, "It is about a search too for daily meaning as well as daily bread, for recognition, as well as cash, for astonishment rather than torpor."

Finding the right paid gig is rarely easy – and it gets harder the more specific your requirements are. I've been especially struck by the challenges several friends faced when seeking work in academia and the non-profit sector. While most found work that serves communities or contributes to the "greater good," for the most part they wound up in roles that diverged from their original interests or that failed to employ the skills and knowledge they had trained in.

And while that can be disappointing, the unexpected roles and workplaces we land in can still prove meaningful. We may find meaning because we are aligned with the organization's mission. We may create meaning by standing up for co-workers or principles, advocating for living wages, encouraging positive workplace practices like diverse hiring practices and sustainability. Engaging through work can mean a lot more than finding the perfect job. As Isao points out, "It's not just what you do it's how you do it that's going to make a difference."

If work is your engagement focus, you'll be well served if you plumb the multitude of books and referral services (e.g. career counseling centers, coaches, online sites) devoted to helping you out. A couple of suggestions are offered below.

Also, don't limit your search to nonprofits. There are plenty of opportunities in business, government, health care and other sectors of the economy.

Here's a small sample of the kinds of roles you might play:

Government: social worker, librarian, planner, city council member, accountant, legislator, researcher, regulator, fire fighter, budget analyst, program assistant, park ranger.

Health and Education: chiropractor, nutritionist, nurse, acupuncturist, public health worker, health navigator, schoolteacher, childcare worker, school bus driver, tutor, lecturer, trainer, professor, researcher.

Communications and The Arts: artist, street theater player, writer, musician, storyteller, photographer, journalist, muralist, radio show producer, political cartoonist, magazine editor, film editor, blogger, programmer, web designer.

Business: permaculture trainer, social entrepreneur, co-op worker, socially responsible investor, solar panel installer, fair trade distributor, fair trade agricultural worker, credit union bank teller, impact investor, publisher.

Nonprofit Sector: The National Center for Charitable Statistics reports there are about 1.5 million nonprofits in the United States. Each of us pictures something different when we hear the word "nonprofit": one person sees a small office with two staff running a legal aid clinic; while another imagines a large university-style cancer research center.

Non-profits play many roles. In June 2016, Idealist.org listed 13,344 available nonprofit jobs organized under the following "areas of focus":

> agriculture, animals, arts, civic engagement, communications access, community development, conflict resolution, consumer protection, crime and safety, disability, disaster relief, drug abuse, economic development, education, energy conservation, environment, family, government reform, health and medicine, housing and homelessness, human rights and civil liberties, human services, immigration, international cooperation, international relations, job and workplace, legal assistance, LGBT, library or resource center, media, men, mental health, microcredit, multi-service agency, museums and history, network of nonprofits, personal finance, philanthropy, politics, poverty and hunger, prison reform, professional association, race and ethnicity, religion and spirituality, research and science, rural, seniors and retirement, social enterprise, sports and recreation, technology, travel and transportation, urban, veterans, victim support, volunteering, women, youth.

Nonprofit Job Examples: shelter advocate, development associate, housing advocate, member services coordinator, administrative assistant, union organizer, volunteer coordinator, donor database manager, residence attendant, event planner, adult education instructor, education and training counselor.

Websites and Books for Engaged Work

Craig's List: Job classifieds internationally includes extensive nonprofit, government, and related job listings: craigslist.org.

Idealist: Extensive nonprofit job listings internationally: idealist.org.

The Foundation Center: A resource center that offers in-depth information on this vast sector: foundationcenter.org.

Melissa Everett's book, *How to Make a Living While Making a Difference.*

Richard N. Bolles's book, *What Color is Your Parachute?*

Do Your Own Thing

You may want to do your own thing:

- Set up a library at your child's school.
- Create a fund to divert profits from your business to a foundation.
- Write a book.
- Organize your apartment building or neighborhood to start recycling or composting or establish a community garden.
- Set up a website to inform people about a cause.
- Design an inexpensive water filter.
- Put on a fundraiser.

One of my favorite examples of this kind of engagement is the Theater of War production my friend Greg Beuthin produced in response to the U.S. invasion of Iraq. He said, "I wanted to consciously use the tools I developed in theater to make the protest against war that other people were making in the street."

The idea came to him while he was walking in the Marin Headlands overlooking the Golden Gate Bridge in the San Francisco Bay Area. It was his birthday on February 11, 2002, and exactly five months following the attack on the World Trade Center. On his walk he noticed an old gun battery on the path, and an outdoor amphitheater. "When I saw this, my very first thought was, wouldn't it be awesome if someone did a Shakespearean antiwar play here," Greg said. A couple of days later he decided to do something himself. He had a partially written play on the Algerian war of independence; he got permission to use the site, and he invited friends who were local writers and actors to participate, ending up with a two-hour-long production of short plays and poetry.

Engage Politically

There are many ways you can engage politically.

You can run for office. To run for federal office, contact the Elections Division at the Secretary of State's office in your state. You need to have resided in your state for a year, and you need to also register with the Federal Elections Commission in Washington D.C. To run for a state office, contact the Elections Division at the Secretary of State's office in your state and find out what the specific filing requirements are for your state. For county level positions–the school board, board of supervisors, transit system, public utilities commission, etc.–contact the County Election Board, and for a position in your city contact the Mayor's Office and ask for the Elections Office.

You can work or volunteer for a political party. If you're not ready to run for office, you might want to get involved in party politics by volunteering or working for one. Call your local party office to learn more. If you volunteer you may end up tabulating, registering voters, walking precincts, working in the office headquarters, fundraising, helping with press releases, designing websites, designing leaflets, phoning party members, or putting on events.

You can advocate and lobby. Another way to become politically involved is to support (or oppose) legislation, ballot initiatives, propositions, and council proposals. You can lend support by writing letters to the editor, talking to public representatives, or working with a nonprofit, union, political party, or any other kind of group that is concerned about the same issue. You can also write legislation and work with the appropriate public official to bring your concern to the local, state, or federal body that would be concerned with it.

Write Letters

You read a blog and see that they've cut funding to local public schools again. This upsets you. You think about writing a letter. Here are a few approaches:

- Write a long, well-researched letter that perfectly expresses what you think and feel.
- Express your opinions and feelings in a few simple sentences, spending ten to fifteen minutes to put together a note that you send off immediately.
- Use a template letter written by an organization that shares your view on an issue, and either copy their words or create a letter that combines what they say with what you want to say.

I'm a big advocate of writing the "easy" letter because I think all too often the letter becomes more than we have the time or patience to write. If you just do it you're more likely to get the letter in the mail and published.

On the other hand, a more thoughtful and thoroughly researched letter will likely have a stronger impact.

Here's the story of someone who made letter writing both a practice and a collective action. Mike Adams started an antiwar letter-writing campaign out of his home just prior to the U.S. invasion of Iraq in 2003. He contacted a bunch of like-minded friends, and they got together to send letters to newspapers all across the country opposing the impending war.

Mike said, "One of the things that I got directly out of writing letters to the editor was that I could read the news on a daily basis and never felt hopeless. I felt empowered when I was writing letters on a regular basis."

This letter-writing campaign was unique because they chose to write letters employing the principles of "nonviolent communication" (NVC), a method of communicating that actively engenders understanding rather than accusations. NVC aims at opening dialog through focusing on your own experience and feelings rather than accusing, blaming and judging the people whom you want to persuade.

Mike had a process. First he wrote a letter that voiced all his anger. "Throw a temper tantrum on pen and paper." He then rewrote each letter using NVC. "Go back through the letter and translate everything into NVC." Mike practices NVC in everyday life as well. "If someone pisses me off at work, I say 'I'm pissed off right now and I'm going to have a tantrum.' And they'll laugh at me. It changes it into something fun."

Elements of a Nonviolent Letter

- Write in a nonjudgmental format.
- Express how the action makes you feel, without directing aggression at the person or organization that upsets you.
- Make a distinction between a request and a demand. Don't demand change, request it.
- Emphasize shared interests.

Where to Send Letters	
The Media	Wikipedia media lists like this one: https://en.wikipedia.org/wiki/List_of_newspapers_in_the_United_States
Elected Officials	USA.gov and Whitehouse.gov
Corporations	**Data Center's** *Researching a Corporation* webpage gives good guidance: twww.datacenter.org/research/corp_res.htm

Engage Online

"Sceptics use words like "clicktavism" to describe political action that demands nothing more of a protester than pressing a button, which may just imply curiosity; and it is rarely possible to prove beyond doubt that e-campaigning is a decisive factor in a political outcome.

"On the other hand, argues Ricken Patel, a cofounder of Avaaz, digital activism rarely ends with the click of a mouse. Avaaz's campaign against the death sentence for adultery imposed on an Iranian woman asks members to phone Iranian embassies (and provides numbers); members are also being urged to put pressure on the leaders of Brazil and Turkey to intercede with Iran. Avaaz is collecting funds for a campaign in the Brazilian and Turkish press, too." –The Economist

Possibilities for online engagement include:

Blogging: Set up your own website or blog on a topic that is important to you. If you like you can allow others to comment on your blog, creating a space for discussion and even action on your issue.

Texting and SMS: In South Africa, my friend Peter worked for CellLife.org where SMS/text messaging is used to help inform and support people who were recently tested for HIV. This service gets information and support to people in rural areas who have access to cell phones but not necessarily computers.

Social networking: "The use of social media is becoming a feature of political and civic engagement for many Americans. Some 60% of American adults use social networking sites like Facebook or Twitter, and a 2012 survey on political engagement by the Pew Research Center's Internet & American Life Project found that 66% of those social media users–or 39% of all American adults–have done at least one of eight civic or political activities with social media."

Online petitions: Check sites that regularly post petitions to sign. IFEX has a "take action" page that regularly posts petitions related to freedom of expression and human rights. To set up your own petition you can use sites like change.org, avaaz.org, or even the U.S. government's "We The People."

Groupware: Meet and organize with others online using groupware tools like Wiggio, Google Drive, and Yahoo groups.

Apps: On the Facebook page "AppsThatActuallyMakeADifference" there are links posted for apps that help you track carbon emissions, screen stocks for ethical investing, make ethical purchases, etc. One app, Copia (www.gocopia.com), helps redistribute food from those who have extra to those who are in need in the San Francisco Bay Area.

Engage Your Ethics/"Green" Your Life

"The Amish...have succeeded simply by asking one question of any proposed innovation, namely: 'What will this do to our community?'"
–Wendell Berry

One type of change work is to attempt to live more in line with your values and beliefs. While this can take many forms, for many this means making an effort to live sustainably, in harmony with the ecology of the planet. This may start with recycling, driving less, conserving water and electricity. For Andy Buckley Bramble and his partner, Amanda, it became a way of life.

They left San Francisco for the New Mexican desert, intending to live off the land and off the grid as much as they could. Before leaving San Francisco Andy said, "When we buy land probably we'll have to do a lot of water catchments and water hauling. The water is going to be our biggest issue in terms of growing our own food. And there's only so much food that we can grow for ourselves; sustainable farming is incredibly hard and time consuming."

I was impressed. They were doing what so many talk about and so few actually attempt.

Sustainability is an "exploration" Andy told me a couple of years after their move. His advice for people seeking to live more sustainably: notice your relationship to all the elements in your life, "Whether it's what sort of structure you're living in or what sort of structure you're building, what sort of food you're putting in your body, or how you're treating yourself and your friends.

"And the other bit is, you know, take it as it comes. Give yourself a break here and there. It's not feasible to just go off into the woods and grow all your own food and that's it. You have to realize that you are in the context of this culture."

I recently made contact with Andy again and was amazed to learn that he and Amanda had done much they originally envisioned. They have a nonprofit now, the Ampersand Sustainable Learning Center. To quote their website:

"Our off-grid site demonstrates sustainable systems including permaculture, land restoration, organic gardening, passive solar design, and wise water techniques. We build with natural and salvaged materials, cook with solar ovens, and rely on rain catchment. Our whole approach to sustainability is about your relationship with your resources. We start with the basics: water, food, shelter, and energy. We are simply gathering, experimenting with, and demonstrating sustainable solutions for living in harmony with our bioregion."

Ampersand is one of many organizations that help people live more sustainably. Here are a few others:

> **Ecology Center:** ecologycenter.org
>
> **Green America**: greenamerica.org, and their **Green Pages**, greenpages.org
>
> **Ecological Footprint:** myfootprint.org
>
> **Transition Towns Network:** transitionnetwork.org

Train to Engage

"If we change internally–disarm ourselves by dealing constructively with our negative thoughts and emotions–we can literally change the whole world"
–The Dalai Lama

"Effective community and institutional change happens when those who serve as agents of transformation understand the foundations of race and racism and how they continually function as a barrier to community self-determination and self-sufficiency." –The People's Institute for Survival and Beyond

Although not a direct form of caretaking or changemaking, a legitimate engagement project would be to take time to nurture and grow your skills, understanding or capacity to engage through any of a variety of possible activities. You may want to take a class, join a support group, sign up for a workshop, or even set aside a period of time for deeper reflection in order to support taking authentic action in the world from the "inside-out." This kind of training and reflection could be your engagement project, or an action step within a project.

We train in order to learn, but also because we want to "be the change" we seek to create in the world (as Mahatma Gandhi so famously put it). Breaking through old patterns of bias linked to race, gender, sexual orientation and other societal differences is one way to do this. At work I recently participated in an "Undoing Racism" training put on by The People's Institute for Survival and Beyond. The People's Institute says that to "undo" racism requires not just advocacy for change but also a willingness on the part of individuals and institutions to examine the root causes of racism - examining how this plays out both personally and collectively. It's through this deeper understanding that behavior patterns change at all levels.

I also took a non-violent communication (NVC) training years ago. NVC is a skill we can develop to express difficult emotions like anger without alienating others or feeling overwhelmed. I went in part to learn how to communicate better with family members and others whose political beliefs strongly diverged from mine. Marshall Rosenberg writes in the book Nonviolent Communication: "NVC guides us in reframing how we express ourselves and hear others. Instead of being habitual, automatic reactions, our words become conscious responses based firmly on an awareness of what we are perceiving, feeling, and wanting. We are led to express ourselves with honesty and clarity, while simultaneously paying others a respectful and empathic attention. In any exchange, we come to hear our own deeper needs and those of others."

Training in compassion can also support our engagement. One of the biggest stumbling blocks in our ability to contribute is our own self-judgement and lack of confidence. My friend Robert Cusick offers Compassion Cultivation Trainings. He says, "Compassion is our willingness to see and accept both sides of ourselves; that which wants relief from suffering, and that which recognizes the causes of suffering and accepts the truth of the way things are - even in the midst of the worldwide climate crisis or our own dying." He says that as our compassion for ourselves and others grows, "we have a much better chance to know what skillful, wise action in the world is called for and possible."

Drop Everything and Engage Completely

"I was describing it to somebody as one of these peak experiences—peak in terms of the rightness of where I am in that moment. Even in the really boring times, just waiting around at a checkpoint or something, there was no place I would rather be at that moment." –Jon Jackson

The last form of engagement relates to following a strong inner need or passion that can take you into situations of adventure, intensity, connection, or conflict, essentially towards something that calls you. My friend Jon Jackson had for a long time felt this need in relation to the situation in Palestine and Israel. He doesn't know why Palestine in particular. He spent years working for a nuclear freeze and later as an anti-apartheid activist. But over the years the issue of Palestinian liberation became more of a concern for him.

Jon and I met in the anti-apartheid movement at UC Berkeley in the early eighties. By day he's a librarian, working at the San Francisco Public Library. But he isn't quiet. At rallies and protests Jon leads people in chants, and he has this way of charming people into joining in, even when they hadn't intended to. We sometimes call him the "mayor of Berkeley" because you can't walk a city block in Berkeley with Jon without someone stopping to give him a hug.

Jon first went to Palestine in 2002 with the International Solidarity Movement (ISM)–an global organization that supports Palestinian and Israeli peace activists. John heard about ISM on the radio. He said, "They were interviewing people who had gotten into [PLO leader Yasser] Arafat's compound when it was under siege by Israeli tanks, and there was another group of people who had come into the Church of the Nativity in Bethlehem around the same time. And the Israeli tanks had besieged it. And the ISM people had gone in with water and supplies and, you know, in essence, just helping them out how they could."

On his first visit to Palestine, Jon's ISM affinity group helped at a Palestinian summer school in the town of Deir Ibzi'a. He and the other volunteers taught classes to school-aged kids there. The following year, Jon wanted to return, but things had worsened. ISM volunteers had been hurt and killed that year. Rachel Corie, a young activist from Portland, Oregon, died while standing in front of a bulldozer that was intent on knocking down the house of a Palestinian. A British ISM volunteer was shot in the head. Jon's desire to go increased; he didn't want to just give in to what he saw as physical intimidation by Israel. He wanted to support the work of ISM.

In the summer of 2003 he took six weeks off from work and flew to the region, not certain if he would even get over the border since the Israeli police were detaining and/or turning back anyone suspected of ISM involvement. He flew to Jordan, then took a bus to Tel Aviv and convinced security police that he wished to visit religious sites. They let him in.

Jon spent a few weeks with the only other ISM volunteer in Rafah, in the Gaza strip, in a part of town where a wall was being constructed to separate Israel and Palestine. A wall that as it rose knocked over the houses of whoever lived in its way. ISM volunteers did not try to stop the construction–after Rachel's death they were regrouping and being cautious. Jon and Laura were there as witnesses and to a certain degree playing a protective accompanying role. When Jon returned to Berkeley, he had photos, videos, and stories. We were all relieved that he was safe.

This was Jon's quest–for it did feel like that level of pull. It was more than activism. There was something personal in Jon's need to go to Palestine. He almost apologizes for this–thinking that maybe he should be more "pure" in his political intentions. But that's what a "call" is; it is that place where the personal and the political meet and we follow our hearts wherever they may lead us.

CONNECTING EXERCISES

1. **Options for action: Use the worksheet below to compare several possible engagement projects.** You'll start with the issue you want to address, then write down the "project" or action you want to engage in related to that concern. Come up with at least three projects ideas.

Issue	Project idea	What I know about this	Potential contacts who can help me engage	What I need to learn to take the next step	Challenges to doing this now	Good reason to do this now

Example:

Issue: *Human Rights* | **Project Idea**: *Volunteer for Human Rights Watch* | **What I Know**: *Just what I've read in the news* | **My Contacts**: *A friend at work with past experience* | **Need to Learn**: *Does HRW have volunteer opportunities?* | **Challenges now**: *I work full time* | **Reason to do this now?** *I've wanted to for a long time and feel motivated.*

2. **Choose a project.** Review the projects you listed in the *Options for Action* exercise and choose one. Do any stand out? Maybe one seems more timely and urgent. This is your engagement project.

3. **Describe your engagement project using the following prompts:**

   - The area issue or need this project addresses.
   - The specific action you will take and/or role you want to play.
   - Any hopes, intentions, or expectations you have related to the kind of contribution you will make.
   - Any hopes, intentions or expectations you have about what your experience will be like.

4. **Reflect on your choice.** What makes this engagement project stand out from any others you may have considered? How are you feeling as you prepare to move into action?

5. **Identify supports and challenges for this project.** Make a list of all the internal and external supports and challenges to doing this project.

Challenges might include procrastination, losing interest early on, not having enough time, not feeling confident about your skills, etc.

Supports might include talking about your engagement with friends, committing engage on a regular basis, reading up on the issue, etc.

6. **Take one small action step to begin your engagement project.** It can be simple. Call a friend and tell them what you've decided to do. Or, make a list of two or three steps you can take in the coming week. Anything that sets this project in motion. "My first small step will be…"

7. **Wait, I'm not ready!** If you're hesitating or strongly conflicted about making a choice right now, then do Plan B instead. Plan B is that you choose a **temporary** engagement project that you will try out for one week. Pretend you're filling in for someone who is out sick this week. Remember to keep it simple. Maybe you'll just do some reading on a topic that interests you. That's a good first step for any project. Remember: you're not making a long-term commitment, you're simply exploring a possibility.

Volunteers Julie and Jim share some learning experiences.

Julie: *All my volunteer experiences have been learning experiences. When I worked at the women's shelter I learned a lot about abuse and how the legal system handles it and how individuals can help address it. I learned at NOW [National Organization for Women] how to organize and what we can do to stop our rights from being abused. And I learned organizational skills, which is very necessary in the volunteer world. I also just learned about what's going on out there and what people are concerned about.*

Interview with Julie Pokrivnak in in San Francisco, California, in 2005, on "Volunteering."

Jim: *I keep thinking: "What can I do with this person? What should I be saying? How can I help? Do they want help?" And then recognizing it's not about my agenda, it's about meeting them in whatever their agenda is.*

Interview Jim Bates and Tim Andres in Woodacre, California, in 2014, on "Hospice Work."

WEEK SIX: LEARN

Listen and learn

Listen and Learn

"Real listening is the ability to let the other person change you."
—Alan Alda

Now that you've set your engagement project in motion, your next step is to deepen your understanding of the problem you're addressing. Talk to and listen to people who have experience and stories to share. Read books and articles on the topic. This chapter offers some ways you can engage in a learning process around your engagement issue.

The five exercises that comprise this chapter are:

- Start with what you know
- Talk with people who know
- Read with a purpose
- Do a "Needs Inquiry"
- Tell the stories

Give this learning some space. Any time spent learning will enable you to engage from a more informed, and more understanding place.

Knowing What You Know

So often we decide not to engage because we think we don't know enough. We think we should already be experts, or at least well versed in a topic before we put ourselves out there. One survey found that most Americans feared speaking in front of an audience more than they did dying or the prospect of nuclear war. We're scared to be wrong, especially in front of other people.

But of course we all start out as beginners. Once upon a time Julia Butterfly Hill didn't know much about redwoods. In fact, she was pretty new to the environmental movement when she climbed up the tree she later named Luna to prevent loggers from clear-cutting California redwoods. She didn't know she was going to stay in Luna for two years—originally she had planned to "tree-sit" for just a few days. Today Julia knows a lot about redwoods and how to save them and her work has inspired others to do the same.

For me, engaging in climate change action was an intimidating prospect. After seeing the film *An Inconvenient Truth*, I was really daunted. When I left the theater I wished I could abandon my car and walk home after learning how much CO2 landed in the atmosphere (for 100 years!) whenever I drove. I was nonplussed at the prospect of getting involved in an issue that required I know something about the weather and how it worked. I wondered how I'd ever be comfortable enough to stand up for, and talk with others about, what had just become my foremost concern.

But I knew a little about global warming when I first began to engage. And you already know something (perhaps quite a lot) about your engagement issue.

Whether you're an expert or a novice, this first exercise is intended to help you freely express yourself on whatever your topic is. An important element of this exercise is that *you don't have to get the facts right* and *you don't have to share what you write with anyone else*. Keeping this in mind will free you up to write honestly and fluidly.

> EXERCISE: Start with What You Know
>
> Take as long as you need to answer the following questions as they pertain to your engagement issue:
>
> What do I already know about this issue? How do I feel about what is happening?
>
> What do I believe are the causes of the situation and most likely solutions?
>
> What do I dislike about the situation?
>
> What do I like about the situation (anything positive)?
>
> How am I directly impacted by or involved in this issue?
>
> Once you are finished, reflect on what you learned. Are you surprised by how much or little you know, or by how strongly you do or do not feel about the situation? Have you seen something you want to explore more?

Who Can You Talk To?

"Over the past thirty years I have found it mindboggling to discover how many people start their own business, at home or elsewhere, without ever first going to talk to anybody who started the same kind of business earlier."
–Richard N. Bolles

Nothing helped me to explore the issue of global warming, and what I might do about it, more than connecting with my friend Karen. Karen knows a lot about the environment, climate activism, and politics. She pointed me to websites and books, and we attended local events together. Later I took a workshop at the Berkeley Ecology Center, where I met weekly with a group of eight others who were all exploring how we could address our personal and collective ecological "footprints."

If you have a "Karen," take full advantage of her good will and knowhow. And if you don't, you'll need to meet some people.

Talking with people who are already involved is the most effective way to learn what's important. Ideally you'll want to talk to people who are **impacted** by your topic, and to those who are addressing it. For example, if you are considering volunteering at a homeless shelter, talk to a homeless person. Ask them what they need. Where do they seek aid? What kinds of help do they seek? What works for them? You'll also want to talk to workers at a shelter. Ask them questions. Listen to them. What important to know? Don't just email, call people. If it makes sense and they have time, meet them in person. As soon as you directly connect with people engaged in your issue, your understanding will expand greatly.

Jerry Brown asked Sister Helen Prejean (best known for her work with inmates on Death Row as depicted in *Dead Man Walking*) what it was like at the housing project where she worked. She said, "The only way you will find the answer to that question is by going to see for yourself. You can hear me talk about it, but I encourage everyone who is scared to death of poor people to find these places–a Hope House, a community center, a drop-in center for the homeless, a soup kitchen– and go there."

Prepare for meetings with people by coming up with some questions beforehand. You can try framing your questions using the old reporting tool of "who, what, where, when, why, how," or structure your questions in some way that will help you make choices about what you want to do, or fill in gaps in what you know.

When you listen to people, you will hear their stories. They will tell you what they care about and why they care. And you are likely to find they care about the same things that you care about.

If you are hesitant to talk to others, I encourage you to consider why, and what might help you get over that hesitation. Sometimes it's because we just want to get started and don't want to take the time. Some of us are shy, while others can't be bothered; we feel we know enough already. If any of this is going on for you, give it a try anyway. It can be especially enlightening to do the things we are most uncomfortable doing.

Human and Indian rights advocate, Alberto Saldamondo said, "One guy in particular, I just enjoy being with. He slows me down. He's an activist. He's been an activist since the day he was born, I think. His name is Jim Main. He lives on the Potomac reservation in Montana. I see him maybe two or three times a year. But his perspective is pretty incredible. He tells stories. He tells me stories. I've stopped asking questions; I just listen to his stories. There's a great wisdom. But I also had to learn how to listen. It's very important to listen, and it's very important to listen to old people."

> **EXERCISE: Two people I can talk to are:** _____ and
> _____.

Read

Read websites, books, journals, blogs, newspapers, news sites. Watch documentaries or even relevant feature films. Listen to radio programs. If you don't know what to read/watch/listen to, ask for suggestions from those who can guide you. Or look for book lists related to your topic. University class websites are great resources for exploring some subjects. Ask a reference librarian for help. Your biggest problem will probably be honing your "reading" down to a manageable collection of materials.

If you are getting a little overwhelmed, try to focus on what interests you, not what you think you *should* be interested in. You also may be attracted to tangents related to your issue. Keep a list of those interests, while staying focused for now on one topic.

> **EXERCISE: Two good things to read are:**
> _____ and _____

Do a Needs Inquiry

"All we have to do is ask 'How can I help?' with an open heart,
and then really listen." –Ram Dass and Paul Gorman

As we learn, we come to understand we are entering an ongoing history of a problem and of ways people have approached it. The roots of the issue may be decades or centuries old. The solutions in play now may have an equally deep and complex history. This needs inquiry tool is intended to help you dig under the surface of the topic. Use the prompts below to the extent that they are relevant to your issue. Skip questions that don't make sense for your engagement:

EXERCISE: Needs Inquiry

What specific or general needs will your engagement project address?

What situation gave rise to these needs? Who is harmed by this situation?

What people or organizations were involved in causing the problem? Have these people in some way benefited from harm caused to others?

Who is responsible for taking care of things? (What person or organization?)

Who is trying to help make things better? What are they doing?

Are you, your family, friends, or community impacted? If so, how?

What would be a good "outcome" of your work or of collective work on this issue?

Tell the Story

"For most of human history, we have been gathering around campfires for light and warmth telling stories. This is the way our history came down to us and also came to include us. This is the way a woman or a man or a child told us what happened to them that day. This is the way one person told of a danger or heard others who experienced it, too, and all could discover that it was not a personal weakness, or that in the telling, there was a shared solution."

–Gloria Steinem

Another way we learn is by telling stories. Telling stories helps us see how one event led to another, culminating in whatever is happening now. We can tell stories to understand different points of views and experiences, or even as a way to break down complexities.

Historian Howard Zinn, author of the popular *A People's History of the United States*, said, "I wanted to tell the story of the nation's wars not through the eyes of the generals and the political leaders but from the viewpoints of the working-class youngsters who became GIs, or the parents or wives who received the black-bordered telegrams. I wanted to tell the story of the nation's wars from the viewpoint of the enemy: the viewpoint of the Mexicans who were invaded in the Mexican War, the Cubans whose country was taken over by the United States in 1898, the Filipinos who suffered a devastating aggressive war at the beginning of the twentieth century, with perhaps 600,000 people dead as a result of the determination of the U.S. government to conquer the Philippines."

You can tell the story of how the 2003 Iraq war began, maybe starting with how George W. Bush was elected, what happened when the planes crashed into the World Trade Center, or what it might have been like for those who escaped, or did not escape. Or you can talk about how people of Middle Eastern descent are being treated today in the U.S., and how that links up with the war.

You can tell a story about the economy, as Adam Davidson did when he so ambitiously set out to explain the complexities of the 2008 subprime mortgage crisis in the radio program that aired on This American Life. Davidson interviewed traders, mortgage brokers, and people who lost their houses, like Richard, a veteran who returned from Iraq and bought a mortgage with an adjustable rate which suddenly shot up one day by $2,000 a month. Davidson even told the story of the mortgages themselves, describing in detail how they were packaged and sold in a way that disguised their true value and concealed the risk.

> **EXERCISE: Tell a Story.** Give it a try. Maybe start with some person you are concerned about. Or group of people. Or describe how it feels to watch what is occurring. Or even try "Once upon a time ..." or "It was a dark and stormy night when..." Anything that will help you start writing creatively.

LEARNING EXERCISES

1. **Reflect** on what you've learned from your work with this chapter. Has it impacted the direction of your project in any way? What more do you want to learn about this area of interest?

2. **Who listens to you?** Listening is an essential part of learning. Who do you know who is a good listener? What makes them good? What characterizes good listening?

3. **Spend a day in silence.** UNPLUG! No Internet, email, phones. Walk around. Listen to the people around you—in cafés, grocery stores, the laundromat. Listen to street sounds and home sounds. What are people saying? How do they feel? What do you hear in their voices? Go hiking and listen to the wind, birds, the sound of walking. Try listening without reacting to everything. Just take it in.

4. **Take your next action steps.** Make a list of actions you'll take to get going on your engagement project. List the steps in order, along with a date by which you want to complete each step. Next list each of the tasks that you need to do in order to complete each step. These tasks should be very specific.

Sample Engagement Plan: *Lower the Carbon Footprint of My Home*

Step 1: Install solar panels   By date: March 1
Task 1: Research options   By date: Jan 15
Task 2: Purchase   By date: Feb 1
Task 3: Have them installed   By date: March 1

Step 2: Install gray-water systems   By date: April 1
Task 1: Research options   By date: March 7
Task 2: Go to outlet with barrels   By date: March 21
Etc.

DEEPENING ENGAGEMENT

Joanna: *The person everyone needs to hear is inside them. I want to help them liberate their own voice so they can hear from themselves what they care about and what they want to do and what they see as possible.*

Louise: *In the field of helping people become the writer that they are, you absolutely have to believe that they have it in themselves. There's no way anybody can put words in someone's mouth and they become a powerful writer. Their voice just doesn't come out that way. It only comes out when things are opened up inside and that allows that person to express what they have to express. People want this very much.*

Joanna: *People want to be real, don't they?*

Louise: *They want to be real and especially when they feel pain for the earth they want to be able to do something. And that's very extreme right now. I have been almost overwhelmed at how many people have come to workshops labeled "Undoing the silence." The term "undoing the silence" really speaks to people because they know that they've experienced silencing and that they're not speaking up. ...You were asking earlier if we don't use the word activist, what do we use? I think I use the word "engage," "involve," "take action."*

Joanna: *I use the word "liberated" a lot. "Liberated into action." That's what we most want to do, is to be part of the healing of our world. That's the deepest desire.*

Interview with Joanna Macy and Louise Dunlap in Berkeley, California, in 2010, on "Facilitating Social Change."

WEEK SEVEN: OPEN

Free your courage

"It is true—I've always loved the daring ones like the black young man who tried to crash all barriers at once, wanted to swim at a white beach [in Alabama] nude." –Alice Walker

"My Soul Is Rested"

One day Martin Luther King was driving to town when he saw a woman walking home from work. He pulled up his car to offer her a ride. The year was 1956 and, like thousands of others that year, she had opted to boycott and walk the miles to and from work rather than step onto a segregated bus. She had already walked seven miles that day. King said to her, "You must be tired." And she responded, "Yes, son, my feets are tired, but my soul is rested."

Before the bus boycott, black Americans had dropped coins into the collection tills of these buses because there appeared to be no other choice. This is how the system worked.

Today we all drop coins into systems we know are bad for us, our communities, and our planet. Whether it's who we work for, what we pay for, or how we do things, we keep dropping those coins.

"I am often frustrated driving my car with petroleum, and seeing hundreds and thousands of other people like me do the same," said my friend Regula. "It's challenging to be so aware of the contribution to the greenhouse effect and be so powerless." When we compromise and participate in systems that are harmful, even violently so to others, we ourselves can feel culpable. Regula rides her bike and walks whenever she can. She also still drives. She's doing the best she can.

After the success of the Birmingham bus boycott, minister Ralph Abernathy realized he had been changed personally by his participation in the boycott. He said in a radio interview, "Once you stop participating with an evil system, you don't want any part of it any more. There was this time when it didn't bother me to go downtown into a segregated waiting room in a bus terminal. ... It didn't bother me to eat in a restaurant that was segregated, but now I cannot. I just cannot. It does something to me."

Around that same time, Mildred Lisette Norman, the year she turned fifty, stepped out of the kind of life we are all familiar with and took up a solo peace walk that lasted for twenty-eight years. She shed her name along with her possessions and called herself Peace Pilgrim. She walked from coast to coast across the United States sharing her visions of inner peace, of a department of peace, opposing war. She established disciplines for herself. For many years she would not accept rides, only walk. She accepted food and shelter from people, but not money. She did not even carry a backpack. Her possessions comprised a comb, a toothbrush, a pen, her correspondence, and copies of her "message:" *"This is the way of peace—overcome evil with good, and falsehood with truth, and hatred with love."*

Why did she do it? Peace Pilgrim described a night which was a turning point in her life. "As I looked about the world, so much of it impoverished, I became increasingly uncomfortable about having so much while my brothers and sisters were starving. Finally I had to find another way. The turning point came when, in desperation and out of a very deep seeking for a meaningful way of life, I walked all one night through the woods. I came to a moonlit glade and prayed. I felt a complete willingness, without any reservations, to give my life—to dedicate my life—to service. "Please use me!" I prayed to God. And a great peace came over me. I tell you it's a point of no return. After that, you can never go back to completely self-centered living. I began to live to give what I could, instead of to get what I could, and I entered a new and wonderful world."

Freedom

What's so wonderful about no possessions? About walking for miles every day in discomfort? About talking with people who don't understand you or think you are crazy? Peace Pilgrim was practicing her own form of freedom: the freedom to live in alignment with her deepest beliefs and her caring for the world.

Freedom is what this chapter is about. The freedom that comes from deep honesty in the ways we show up in the world. This week, be a little more brave than usual. Extend yourself to speak up and stand up for your truth. Stretch your boundaries and habitual patterns. And, continue to move forward with your engagement project in whatever ways you need to: learning, connecting, investigating. Keep taking little steps.

You can explore acting freely by working with these three practices:

Speak up: Speak up about what you care about, whether over dinner with friends, or calling your opinion into a talk show, or sharing information that matters with people in power. Say what you believe in or care about, even if your views are not popular.

Stand up: Be willing to lead when a situation calls for it, openly acting on your convictions–not shirking when the need for action arises.

Give up: Let go of habits and ways of doing things that you don't believe in, or that you know are harmful to the environment, other beings, people, and your conscience.

Each time we speak up, stand up, or give up, we exercise our freedom, power, and courage. As we align our actions to our beliefs we reap many benefits like:

Community. We get to meet and hang out with others who share our values and concerns.

Being at peace with the world. When we prioritize facing the world's needs, we are more at peace in our relationship to the world.

Empowerment and learning. Any time we face our fears of doing what matters most we experience our own power and we remember why it is important to take risks for what we care about.

Respect for self and others. When we do the right thing we respect ourselves more.

Enjoyment and interest. Our courageous engagement is an adventure which is often fun and nearly always interesting.

What's more, we free ourselves from constriction, guilt, denial, frustration, fear, bad behavior (sometimes), and resentment (towards others or ourselves for not doing more). "Between stimulus and response, there is a space," wrote Viktor Frankl wrote in Man's Search for Meaning. "In that space is our power to choose our response. In our response lies our growth and our freedom."

When we are courageous we give ourselves the bounty of living from a more true, real, and connected place.

Speak Up

"The brain is a remarkable thing. It starts to function the instant you are born and doesn't stop until the moment you get up to speak." –Jacob M. Braude

Sharing our political views, our ideas about right and wrong, our fears and hopes–all can be very scary. This can be true whether we're talking to a friend over dinner or to a room full of strangers. When we speak, our egos are on the line. One wrong word and a friendly situation can turn into one of enmity. We can make fools of ourselves, or wind up in conflicts with people we care about. No wonder we're cautious.

"Self-disclosure may be as scary to you as skydiving without a parachute. You hold back because you anticipate rejection or disapproval. But you miss a lot. Self-disclosure makes relationships exciting and builds intimacy. It clarifies and enlivens. Without self-disclosure, you are isolated in your private experience," write Matthew McKay, Martha Davis, and Patrick Fanning in *How to Communicate*.

Speaking up can be a practice in personal truth telling, or a willingness to raise uncomfortable or unfair dynamics with coworkers and neighbors, or sharing information and concerns about something taking place in the public sphere.

When people speak up they free others to do so as well. The Berkeley Free Speech Movement emerged in 1964 when students and faculty opposed a university's attempt to control the distribution of political literature on campus. When activist Jack Weinberg was arrested and placed in a police car for distributing literature, students quickly surrounded the car and staged a spontaneous sit-in—keeping the car there (with Weinberg in it) for over thirty hours.

That day, speech after speech was made by students who stood on top of the car. Amongst them was Bettina Apthecker, who was one of the few visible women leaders in that movement. "My first speech was from the top of the police car. … It was Thursday, October 1, 1964. I had just turned twenty."

Apthecker's courage and leadership inspired other women in all kinds of ways. She said, "Years later I learned that there were women who left abusive marriages because they saw me on television; women decided to speak up in their classes or to say what they really thought to a male companion or lover because they heard me speak at a rally on Sproul Hall steps. Some women decided to leave their jobs in search of more meaningful work; others returned to school; others joined the union or the peace movement, deciding that they too could act."

The movement prevented the university's attempt to suppress free speech. And in so doing it transformed UC Berkeley into a symbol of free speech to this day.

Whistle

And then there are whistle-blowers. Consider Daniel Ellsberg, who in 1971 made public a secret and classified document that became known as the Pentagon Papers. The report - which few knew existed at the time - brought to light deceit and misinformation spread by the Office of the President over several administrations regarding the Vietnam War, including a bombing campaign of Laos, Cambodia, and other parts of Southeast Asia, which was kept secret from the public at large.

Ellsberg confronted with great courage the possibility of spending a hundred years in prison for this famous act of whistleblowing. He also lost the approval of old friends and colleagues who were shocked by his betrayal and his vocal shift in viewpoint about a war he had once believed in.

He hoped that by making the report public, policymakers would immediately end the Vietnam War in light of the new information. They did not. While his action had many ripple effects (including inspiring other whistle blowers), he does not credit it with helping end the war.

In November 2015, the National Security Agency whistleblower, Edward Snowden, met Daniel Ellsberg, along with Arundhati Roy and John Cusack, in Moscow. Roy reports that Snowden said that day, "If we do nothing, we sort of sleepwalk into a total surveillance state where we have both a super-state that has unlimited capacity to apply force with an unlimited ability to know (about the people it is targeting)—and that's a very dangerous combination. That's the dark future."

> **EXERCISE: Self-censorship.** In what contexts do you
> tend to censor yourself and why? Does this ever relate to
> sharing social and political views? Write about this and/or
> share about this issue with friends. Explore what could help
> you to speak up more in ways that would be effective and
> perhaps not so scary.

Stand Up

"Courage is contagious. If you take a courageous step as an individual you will literally change the world. You should never doubt your ability to change the world." –Glenn Greenwald

"Get up, stand up, stand up for your rights! Get up, stand up, don't give up the fight!" –Bob Marley

2011 was a year of "standing up," as evidenced by the Arab Spring, the OCCUPY Movement, and more. The Arab Spring was said to have begun when Mohamed Bouazizi, a Tunisian street vendor, set himself on fire in protest over his ill treatment by municipal authorities. This tragic act resulted in a series of demonstrations against the government, which in turn led to the flight of the Tunisian president from the country after twenty-three years of rule, and the nation's first democratic elections. The Tunisian experience in turn inspired protests for justice and democracy throughout the Middle East and beyond.

To be visible, to be vocal, to support, to lead are all ways we "stand up." We stand up for ourselves, for others, for a cause. We stand up by participating–by going to meetings and rallies. We stand up by responding when people need help. Standing up often means leading. It can mean stepping in when a need for leadership arises, even if we'd rather not.

Tim DeChristopher spontaneously stood up to the Bush Administration. In 2008, the Bush administration put "environmentally protected" land parcels up for bid to oil and gas speculators. A small group of activists showed up at the parcel auction to protest. Tim DeChristopher, a protester, found himself mistaken for one of the bidders and spontaneously decided to walk into the auction, bidding number in hand. He thought he might make a statement about global warming if the opportunity arose. Instead, he started bidding.

When authorities later learned he didn't have the money to purchase the parcels he had won, he was tried and sentenced to prison for two years. This was an unusually harsh sentencing for an act of civil disobedience.

At his sentencing in 2011, DeChristopher said, "This is a case about the right of citizens to challenge the government. Those who are inspired to follow my actions are those who understand that we are on a path toward catastrophic consequences of climate change. They know their future, and the future of their loved ones, is on the line. And they know we are running out of time to turn things around."

Standing up happens in many ways. It's when we volunteer for that PTA committee, or involve ourselves in mediating a conflict between coworkers, or when we step in to accompany or help guide a friend in emotional difficulty.

Human rights lawyer Alberto Saldamando suggests we stand up for our communities. "It really is not what you win from the other side, but what you win for your own. Like the American Indian movement. It's much more important that Indians know they have a right and act in accordance with that right, than it is for the government to recognize it. Because once you act in a self-determined manner, then the government has to deal with it."

On YouTube there are many short video clips of citizens standing up to authorities with the use of their cell phones. In one clip a man answers the door to police with his cell phone video camera running. They ask him to turn it off so they can come in to conduct a search for someone. He refuses both requests, and tells them that he is at that moment sending video of the interaction directly to YouTube. He requests ID from them, and then asks for their search warrant to enter his premises. He tells them the man they are looking for isn't there. When the officers insist, he says, "You're at my door with guns and I fear for my life." They eventually give up and leave.

Cameras are popping up in all kinds of situations: traffic stops, arrests, border patrol checkpoints, and protests. Armed with knowledge of their constitutional rights and the cameras, ordinary citizens are watching and logging interactions with authorities both in the hopes of capturing the truth and preventing harm.

> **EXERCISE: Stand up.** Write about or describe a time when you stood up for a person, cause, or belief. Write also about how you feel when you stand up for what you care about.

Give Up

"Future generations may find it incomprehensible that people, particularly in industrialized countries, continued until well into the twenty-first century to engage in behavior that seriously compromised the habitability of their own countries and the planet."–American Psychological Association, "Psychology and Global Climate Change," 2010

My friend Noel, a vegan and animal rights advocate, sometimes longs for feta cheese. Gandhi famously gave up sugar when a little boy asked about sugar being bad for his teeth; he gave up sweets so he could advise the child to do so as well. The Dalai Lama doesn't take baths: to conserve water, he only showers.

David Gershon, author of *Low Carbon Diet*, makes this straightforward case for lowering our carbon footprint:

"Global warming is changing the world.

"The primary cause of global warming is carbon dioxide emitted into the atmosphere through the burning of fossil fuels.

"The typical American household generates 55,000 pounds of carbon dioxide annually.

"If you're among those who understand the seriousness of our plight, you probably feel called to do something about it.

"In just a single month you can ... reduce your CO_2 footprint by at least 5000 pounds."

There are boundless opportunities for giving things up to better ourselves and the world, especially in a society that pushes us to indulge our basest desires with no visible benefits beyond instant gratification. Food, transportation, energy use, our money, our time, our ways of treating others, even attitudes and worldviews are all possible avenues for positive change.

Sometimes letting go is easy, but often we might feel as if we have to relinquish something we're not sure we're ready to give up. The American Psychological Association's "Psychology and Global Climate Change" report found that "Many habitual behaviors are extremely resistant to permanent change (e.g., eating habits), and others are slowly changed (e.g., use of seat belts). Ensconced habits do not change without a substantial push."

Letting go can require that we face uncomfortable truths about our ability to make changes that might look relatively easy, but turn out to be daunting. One challenge I've faced has been to drive less as a way to lower my carbon footprint. There isn't much public transportation where I live, so my challenge has been to use my bike more. One day I examined my blocks related to getting on the bike and realized that what was stopping me was one very long, steep hill. I was physically afraid of biking down that hill on the one hand, and also worried that I wouldn't do so well going back up that hill on my way home.

Finally, I realized I couldn't write this chapter and not at least try. So I did. I biked to town, visited the library, went to the store, and then to the bike shop. I had a great time. And it felt wonderful. I was scared at times and I did have to walk the bike uphill for a while on my way back, but that wasn't so bad. And it didn't take nearly as long as I'd imagined.

Giving something up–especially when no one is forcing us or helping us–can require a combination of will power, effort, and commitment. If you don't really feel the need to make a personal change, no matter how harmful your actions are you are not going to change. Conviction carries us into action.

How Much to Give (Up)

I work part-time at a Buddhist meditation center where we offer residential retreats. At the end of each retreat the participants are offered a chance to give dāna–donations–to the teachers and to some of the staff whose livelihood comes from what is given. As we describe this dāna system to the participants, the advice is often: "Give enough so that you feel generous, but not so much that you regret it and feel like you have given too much."

Perhaps this same principle can be applied to how we give *up*. Don't give up so much that you regret or resent your choices. Don't give up everything at once. Give up what you are ready to let go of–or perhaps almost ready to let go of, then take it from there.

A memorable story of giving (up) is that of millionaire Zell Kravinsky, who, as reported in the *New* Yorker in 2004, "had given almost his entire 45-million-dollar real-estate fortune to charity," and who felt this wasn't enough. He decided to donate a kidney to a woman he didn't know. Zell Kravinsky said, "It seems to me crystal clear that I should be giving all my money away and donating all of my time and energy." *New Yorker* reporter Ian Parker wrote, "He speculated that failure to be this generous was corrosive, in a way that most people don't recognize. 'Maybe that's why we're fatigued all the time,' he mused–from "the effort" of disregarding the great needs of others."

OPENING EXERCISES

1. Feeling free.

   I feel free when _____

   I feel constrained when _____

   A time in my life I felt especially free was when _____

   A time in my life I felt very constrained was when _____

2. **Letting go.**

   I wish I could let go of these objects _____

   I wish I could let go of these habits _____

   I wish I could let go of these situations or activities _____

   I also wish I could let go of _____

3. **I would love to give.**

   I wish I could give these friends better health: _____

   I wish I could give these communities more resources _____

   I wish I could give these friends more happiness_____

   I wish I could give myself more: _____

   I wish I could give the planet more: _____

   I wish I could give humanity more: _____

4. **Living with compromises.**

   List three ways you'd like to contribute or engage that would really stretch you. Also, list what you do now in relationship to that. For example, I know my footprint on the world would be better if I were to let go of my car. But in the meantime I have settled for watching how fast and how often I drive.

Ways I'd Like to Contribute or Engage	What I Have Settled On for Now

5. **Living with compromises, Part II.**

   So much of what we do in life seems to result in both good and harm. Fill out the "negatives" and "positives" you associate with paying taxes, driving a car, buying food, etc. Feel free to add to the list.

	Negatives	Positives
Paying taxes		
Driving a car		
Buying food		

   My government supports my freedom by: _____

   My government limits my freedom by: _____

6. **Leadership.** Take note of gaps in leadership in your life at work or school. Are there important issues that people are talking about but not acting on? Can you imagine taking the lead on these issues? Why or why not?

7. **Engagement Project Check-in:** How is your engagement project progressing? Freewrite about it and check in with a friend. What have you done so far? What are your next steps?

Tempel: *I went to a Nevada nuclear test site with a group of friends. We saw people committed to nonviolence there. I was moved by three Quaker women who were arrested. There was no anger in them. They lived in a place of joy applying their joyous hearts to ending nuclear war. I saw them as role models, but didn't know how to transform myself. It wasn't until my first silent meditation retreat that I found the heart/mind to do the work I wanted to do.*

Intensive service or intensive activism is a deep training in showing up, being motivated by our highest ideals. We train in how to connect with people whether we're tired or happy. It's a great training ground. You can burn out, but it calls upon you very deeply—usually on your heart.

Interview with Tempel Smith in Woodacre, California in 2012, on "Engaged Buddhism."

WEEK EIGHT: REFLECT

Reflect, integrate, and keep on engaging

"It claims no special powers and arises in small discrete ways, like blades of grass after rain. The movement grows and spreads in every city and country, and involves virtually every tribe, culture, language, and religion from Mongolians to Uzbeks to Tamils. It is composed of families in India, students in Australia, farmers in France, the landless in Brazil, the Bananeras of Honduras, the "poors" of Durban, villagers in Irian Jaya, indigenous tribes of Bolivia, and housewives in Japan."
–Paul Hawken

Graduation

While the emphasis throughout this book has been on making one *small* difference, there's a *big* difference between acting and doing nothing. And you did it. You stepped into action and now the world gets to benefit from your care.

It's a big deal that you've become one of the actors instead of one of the bystanders. And that you did so despite all the reasons not to. You have been able to push through other priorities, or apathy, or overly grandiose ideas, or whatever other stumbling blocks made getting here a little challenging.

While I've worked on this book off and on over the years, people kept saying to me "It's so needed now!" I think this kind of book has always been timely. But I also believe especially now.

This is a remarkable time as you know. Poverty, war, climate change, racial injustice, repression, mass migration… We feel the stresses. None of us can imagine how the conflicts we are caught up in are going evolve in the coming years. Collectively we face enormous systemic challenges that need to be addressed in the context of poorly functioning political machinery, an economic system that seems hostile to the poor and the earth, and a civil society that lacks a coherent vision and means of organizing. And things are moving fast.

Your completion of this workbook marks a graduation of sorts into a community of engagers. Paul Hawken describes us as being part of a movement which is "humanity's immune response to resist and heal the effects of political corruption, economic disease, and ecological degradation." In this community we all help one other along. We turn to each other for encouragement, support and inspiration. Doing this together we face what is before us knowing that no one person carries the burden alone.

Reflection

"A pause is a suspension of activity, a time of temporary disengagement, when we are no longer moving toward any goal. The pause can occur in the midst of almost any activity and can last for an instant, for hours, or for seasons of our life."
–Tara Brach

This final chapter offers a framework that you can use to reflect on how your engagement project is working out for you. Maybe the time to reflect is now and maybe it won't be for another few weeks or months. Or perhaps it's something you'll do at intervals.

Reflection serves two purposes. On the one hand we look up from our work and simply notice what we have been doing. We notice both as the neutral observer–"Wow, I spent a lot of time on this project"–and we notice in our hearts and bodies how it has felt to take part: "Humph, this has been quite difficult at times." On the other hand we reflect in order to evaluate and assess. Is this project going well? Is there something that needs to change? Several prompts are offered to help guide you in this evaluation and review:

- Make a list of what you've done
- Confirm what's going well
- Confirm what's not working
- Affirm your impact
- Consider what needs to adjust

Make a List

Take out a blank piece of paper or set up a new document on the computer, and just make a list of all you've done. Nonprofits do something like this every year when they churn out annual reports for their donors. American Civil Liberties Union (ACLU) president Anthony Romero wrote in their 2014 report, "An annual report by definition is a review of the year's achievements, but I also see it as a source of inspiration. Defeating the discriminatory Defense of Marriage Act in the U.S. Supreme Court last year, for example, gave us the momentum to chalk up over forty court victories for the freedom to marry."

When I make lists like this I usually learn that I've been doing more than I thought. Your list may shake out memories of meetings, email exchanges, or the different ways you helped out at an event. There's an accumulation of many, often forgotten, little tasks that make up our engagement projects and today they get to be counted.

EXERCISE: The List.

Right now, without grading or judging yourself, make a list of what you've done—i.e., specific activities—as part of your engagement project since you started this workbook, or for whatever time interval makes sense to you.

Include in this list the big and the small; everything counts. The list doesn't have to be long. You just want to take an honest look at what you've been up to.

What's Going Well

"The reward, the real grace, of conscious service, then, is the opportunity not only to help relieve suffering but to grow in wisdom, experience greater unity, and have a good time while we're doing it."
—Ram Dass and Paul Gorman

It is so easy not to look up and notice all the good that comes along with engaging in change and service work. As somebody said, the mind is sticky like Velcro when it comes to dwelling on all the negative things we experience and like Teflon when it comes to the positive.

What's been good about your engagement experience? What do you most appreciate about it? Hopefully you feel nourished by your project. You may even feel like it's a privilege or honor to be in your role. Positive experiences of engaging can be:

- Feeling inspired
- Loving what we do
- Connecting with others
- Feeling good about what we offer
- Being part of a community
- Learning new skills
- Feeling the work is meaningful

My mom delivers meals to homebound elderly people for the non-profit Meals on Wheels. She enjoys chatting with those she delivers meals to, knowing that many of them appreciate the simple human contact she brings along with the food. She likes that this is part of her weekly routine in her retirement. She loves that she can support an organization that enabled her own elderly mother to live at home a couple of years longer than would otherwise have been possible.

Jim Bates describes his hospice volunteer experience as profound. He says, "When you're sitting with somebody who's dying, it's different from most of what you've done in your life. It's an invaluable experience."

Organizer Ken Paff told Studs Terkel in *Hope Dies Last*, "We started out to change the union, and we ended up changing ourselves."

Whether you simply feel good about showing up regularly, or are excited by the new things you are learning, or have a deep sense of fulfillment, it's important to affirm the different ways you are benefiting from your engagement work.

EXERCISE: What's good? Write a paragraph or two on what you most value about your engagement work personally, intellectually, emotionally, and/or spiritually. What has been especially positive for you? What do you feel good about?

What's Not Working

What's not going so well? If you've been working on your project for a few weeks or months now, you may have had some unpleasant experiences along with the good ones. Most engagement work is a mixed bag and acknowledging what is not working is as important as acknowledging what's going well.

Challenging experiences can include:

- Feeling we aren't very effective

- Unhappiness with interpersonal dynamics
- Feeling unappreciated
- Not feeling inspired enough
- Being overworked and stressed out

I've been especially struck by the experience of nurses, who speak of loving their work, feeling good about what they do, connecting with patients, and comradery with coworkers. And those same nurses describe also being treated poorly by patients and coworkers, feeling like they are treated as cogs in the machine of the hospital, and experiencing long hours, burnout, and worse.

The negatives don't have to be a big deal, but we do want to pay attention to them, as very often they are obstacles we can work with.

> **EXERCISE: What's difficult?** Make a list of any challenges you are experiencing in your engagement work. Do these challenges outweigh the good experiences? How might you work with them to improve your situation?

Affirm Your Impact

"Our efforts at altruism have a mixed record of success at helping others, but they have an almost perfect record of helping ourselves."
–Nicholas D. Kristof

If you didn't feel you were having some kind of positive impact, it's very unlikely you'd show up to work on your project. We're here to make a difference and we do. Usually there's no finish line or final outcome—there's just showing up, doing our best, and from time to time getting a glimpse of the fruits of our actions.

Martin Luther King, Jr., said, "A final victory is an accumulation of many short-term encounters. To lightly dismiss a success because it does not usher in a complete order of justice is to fail to comprehend the process of achieving full victory."

Our effectiveness is apparent in all kinds of ways. It can be the full house at the event we helped with. The official we campaigned for got elected. The kids we tutored got better grades and are enjoying school more. The movement we joined brought about a shift in policy.

Sometimes we learn we have an impact because people tell us they were moved or inspired by or affected by our work.

We know we have an impact when we ourselves feel good about our efforts, or when we recognize we've learned something.

No matter how small or big, affirm the good things that result from the work you do as an individual, or as a member of a larger group. It all counts.

> **EXERCISE: Write about ways you know your engage-
> ment project is having a positive impact on:**
>
> Yourself: _____
>
> Specific people or beings:_____
>
> A community: _____
>
> A cause: _____

Adjustments

Most engagers I know struggle to find the right balance of time and energy to give to their project. Those who give too much are often stressed and overburdened. Those who give too little often express frustration or feelings of guilt or inadequacy; they want to do more but feel held back or unclear about what to do.

Balanced engagement is unique to each of us. For some balance means engaging is at the center of their lives. For others it means volunteering a couple of hours a month. I received an email from Katie recently. She cares about climate change, but expressed concerns about joining our

Green Group at work. "Though I am passionate about the topic, I am extremely limited in time. But I want to make an effort, so here it goes. Keep me in the loop, and I'll do my best."

For environmentalist Larry Gibson, balance meant giving everything to his cause. "I never wanted to become an activist, but I had to. If I hadn't I would have been torn off this mountain a long time ago. There are thousands of people around the world who have heard me speak since I started this work, but honestly I wish to God no one knew my name. I wish I didn't have to leave my home and talk to people about mountaintop removal. Last year I traveled eight months out of the year talking to people about this stuff. But I know I have to bring this message to the world and I'm going to fight for justice in every way I can."

We recognize balance as a feeling of being at peace with our efforts; things are on track we're doing what we need to be doing. My mom is completely satisfied with her level of engagement with Meals on Wheels. Every Wednesday she delivers meals for two to three hours. Perhaps part of her satisfaction results from the rhythm of showing up each week at the same time of day. Also, she just feels good about the work she's doing.

Balanced action is authentic. Buddhist teacher Jack Kornfield sometimes tells this favorite story: "A school principal used to make sandwiches for the many homeless people in her neighborhood. Several days a week, when she got home from school, if she was not too tired, she would go to her kitchen and make several dozen sandwiches. She took pleasure in preparing and distributing this food. She didn't care if she was thanked for it or mind if her offering was refused. She was doing it because it simply felt right to do.

"After some time, the local media found out about her after-school activity, and she became a minor celebrity in her area. Inspired by her work, other teachers and friends began to send her money for her ministry. To their surprise they all received their money back with a short note that read, 'Make your own damn sandwiches.'"

As mentioned in the last chapter, balanced giving (or engaging) occurs when we offer enough of ourselves or our resources that we feel the impact of our contribution, but not so much that by giving we harm ourselves emotionally or materially.

EXERCISE: Which of the following rings most true for you? Engaging in service or changemaking is:

One of many interests

Part of my spiritual practice

Part of my work

Important in my life

Essential in my life

At the center of my life

Integration

"It seems to me that, as a contemplative, I do not need to lock myself into solitude and lose all contact with the rest of the world; rather, this poor world has a right to a place in my solitude."

–Thomas Merton

A few years ago the phrase "Climate Action as Practice" came to mind as I pondered how to prioritize both my meditation practice and engaging the climate crisis. Recognizing that I expected to be engaging in climate change action for a very long time, I wondered if there was a way I could make action on climate a form of practice. What would that look like?

A new workshop emerged from this question: *One Small Planet: Climate Action as Practice.* The workshop attracted people who, like me, were looking for a similar balance between action in the world and inner stability. One participant signed up for the class so he could take action on climate "from the inside out." Another shared at the end that as a result of the workshop she now had "tools that I can always refer back to and use to deepen my climate engagement in a practical and authentic way." Each week we worked with a different mindfulness practice that helped us focus our attention on the climate crisis in a way that wasn't overwhelming.

Many people turn to meditation and mindfulness practices to find balance and centering. We know meditation works because we feel better (more whole, more balanced) when we do it. It's clear that meditation supports us. This is of course true of other spiritual practices as well.

What may be less obvious is that focusing on and engaging in social action can also center us internally. When we turn purposely towards the issues that concern us we absorb what's happening not just in the abstract (i.e., intellectually), but in our hearts and bodies as well. It's when we turn away from the difficulties that concern us that we stress out. When we focus on the reality of our world situation, we enter a more real and honest relationship with it.

> **EXERCISE: Mindfulness in Action.** For one week take twenty minutes a day to do a simple meditation practice. Begin each practice by focusing your attention on the engagement issue that is most present for you right now. For example, if it relates to racism, begin your meditation by first closing your eyes, focusing on the breath as best you can. Then after a minute or so, purposely bring your attention to racism in whatever ways that is most apparent to you. Notice what images arise and what stories arise. Try to allow yourself to be present with how your body, thoughts, and emotions shift and change when you bring this into focus. If there's sadness, notice sadness. If anger, notice anger. If you feel nothing, notice that. The important thing is not to judge yourself for any thoughts or feelings as you bring this awareness in. You just want to "befriend" this area of concern and start to notice how it is landing in you. If your thoughts drift off, that's OK too. After a minute or so you may well lose focus. In that case just rest your attention on the breath.

Keep Coming Back

"Consciously or unconsciously, every one of us does render some service or another. If we cultivate the habit of doing this service deliberately, our desire for service will steadily grow stronger, and it will make not only for our own happiness, but that of the world at large."
—Mahatma Gandhi

"Maybe we do look—really look—but then, inevitably, we seem to forget. Remember and then forget again. Climate change is like that; it's hard to keep it in your head for very long. We engage in this odd form of on-again off-again ecological amnesia for perfectly rational reasons. We deny because we fear that letting in the full reality of the crisis will change everything. And we are right."
—Naomi Klein

At the beginning of the book I suggested you find an object that could act as a reminder of your intention to engage. That's because we need reminders. It doesn't take long for a great idea or inspiration to lose its shine. The flash of brilliance passes, and we are left with the work but missing perhaps that fresh raw intensity that spurred us to action in the first place. We can forget that what once felt urgent is still important. And in forgetting, we can lose energy and interest.

It's good to keep committing to what we care about. One of the wisest things anyone ever told me was in a Yin Yoga class—a practice that involves staying in poses for several minutes at a time. She said that when we think we need to move out of an uncomfortable posture, sometimes that's when we most need to stay; moving away from pain can mean moving away from an opportunity to grow. When we can stay in those places of discomfort we may find release and insight, or a deeper understanding of what's hard about staying. Sometimes staying just another day, week, or month may lead to resolution and deeper engagement.

Ironically, part of what allows us to keep engaging is taking the occasional (or more than occasional) break, or sometimes moving onto something new. While some people volunteer for decades at the same library or halfway house, others may take up an interest for a year or two and then move on to the next thing. It's completely natural that engagements come and go. There are life cycles to the work we do. Alberto spoke of committing to a project for a few years then needing to shift to something new so he wouldn't burn out. Julie left the women's shelter after volunteering for a year and a half. "They had a high turnover rate because it was stressful and people don't tend to do it long term. You can't be in that kind of situation long term."

Renewal

"One of the metaphors that my daughter and I use a lot is the drop in the bucket. We're just a drop in the bucket, and that's meaningless. But we say, 'No, wait a minute. If you have a bucket, those raindrops fill it up very fast. Being a drop in the bucket is magnificent.' The problem is we cannot see the bucket. Our work is helping people see that there is a bucket. There are all these people all over the world who are creating this bucket of hope. And so our drops are incredibly significant." –Frances Moore Lappé

It was unexpectedly hot when I was away from home for a few days one fall. A pot of yellow daisies I'd left outside on the porch had wilted and dried up. They seemed on the verge of death. I felt terrible. With little hope, I brought the pot of flowers inside and doused them with water. A lot of water! And after a couple of days, half of the withered flowers actually started to fill out again as if they hadn't been nearly burned to a crisp.

In 2014, David signed up for an online *One Small Planet* workshop. He was one of three men on the call who were all returning to environmental engagement after having burned out or moved on many years previously. Now, with the rise of the climate movement and the glaring urgency of the situation, they were back.

David told us on the first class call that he was quite sick and that this might interfere with his ability to participate. As it turned out, it was the only call he made. He died about two weeks later. Here is what he shared about his reasons for taking the workshop:

"I have a teenage daughter who is about to head off to college. [Climate change] is one of the last things on her mind. She's a great kid. Part of it is, even in my simplest of relationships, how to teach people to care without a focus on guilt, fully well recognizing this has a profound effect on her future whether she realizes it or not.

"The other part for me personally, I'm in a different place in my own life. So as far as this workshop, I'm not sure. If my health improves–and I'm definitely open to that possibility, and it's definitely against the odds–I could imagine becoming somewhat of an activist again. Maybe part of it is also trying to find ways in which I can use my spiritual practice. And if nothing else, just my prayers and compassion for the world might be about the main thing I can do right now. But I want to do what I can do."

REFLECTING EXERCISES

1. Meditate.

   Close your eyes.

   Focus your attention on your breathing. If you like, focus especially on the breath where it flows through your nostrils.

   Breathe. When a thought or feeling or image arises, notice it but do not latch on, just return to focusing on the breath.

   Do this for five or ten minutes.

2. **Spend time with the earth.**

   Walk. Walk in the city or the country. Walk for the sake of walking, not to get anywhere, not for your health, just to walk.

   Garden. There is something about actually touching and playing with soil that brings us close to the earth. Get dirty. Dig holes in the ground. If you don't have a garden or place to dig, buy some potting soil and plant some seeds or starters in pots. Smell the earth.

   Write. Write about the ocean, mountains, trees, the wind, or any other part of nature that appeals to you. Consider your relationship to what you write about. What connects you to the ocean or to trees?

   Draw. Draw the ocean, mountains, trees, wind. Use crayons, watercolors, or pastels. Enjoy the feeling of drawing.

3. **What you've learned.** Reflect on what have you done and what have learned since you began this Workbook.

4. **How it's going.** Reflect on how your engagement is going right now. Are you enjoying it? Does the project feel fulfilling? What do you enjoy most/least about the project?

5. **Self-care.** Write about ways you take care of yourself now as you engage. How might you take even better care of yourself?

6. **Appreciate all those who have supported you doing this engagement work.** Make a list or write a paragraph of all those who helped you or made it possible for you to engage.

7. **Remember why you are doing this work.** Remember the intention you set at the beginning of the book. Would you renew this intention now or do you have a new intention now that you've set the project in motion?

My Wishes for You

Be inspired

Feel your connection to the world

Know that you are an equal partner in the world and that your actions and choices matter

Be confident in expressing your concerns and hopes for the world

Take risks as you face those concerns

Be at peace with your limitations

Take care of yourself no matter what

Just be yourself

Issue Keywords

These issue keywords are used in the Bay Area Progressive Directory (bapd.org)

abortion rights addiction adoption & foster care advertising affirmative action Afghanistan Africa African Americans ageism agriculture AIDS / HIV air alcohol Algeria anarchism animal liberation animal shelters and adoption antisemitism Appalachia appropriate technology Arab Americans Arabs architecture Argentina Armenian Americans art Asia Asian Americans assistive technology at-risk youth Australia automobiles autonomy Balkans banks Berbers bicycling biodiesel biodiversity biofuels bioregionalism biotechnology bisexuals black lives matter blogs books boycotts Brazil brownfields Burma business Cambodia Cambodian Americans campaign finance reform Canada cannabis capitalism caregiver support Caribbean carpools censorship Central America chemical weapons Chicanas / Chicanos child abuse child labor childcare children Chile China CIA / FBI / NSA circumcision civil disobedience civil liberties civil rights class classes / courses climate change climate justice clothing coalitions coastal environment cohousing collectives Colombia colonialism comics commodification communications communism Community Supported Agriculture community-building composting computers conflict resolution conscientious objectors conservation conspiracy consumer lifestyle consumer protection Contract with America control control techniques cooperative living cooperatives copyright coral reefs corporate-controlled globalization corporations Costa Rica counseling county government covert operations crafts creativity credit unions creek restoration crime criminal justice Cuba cultural survival culture jamming cycling dams death penalty debt cancellation decentralization deforestation delivery democracy demographics demonstrations depleted uranium deregulation desert developing world development direct action disabilities disasters discrimination distribution of wealth diversity divestiture domestic violence draft / registration drugs Earth Day East Timor eating disorders ecology economic conversion economic globalization economic justice economic sanctions economics Ecuador editorial comment education educational curriculum educators El Salvador elections electromagnetic radiation electronic commerce elitism email mailing lists eminent domain employee ownership employment endangered species / habitat energy environmental justice Eritrea Europe facilitation fair trade family family court farmers markets fascism fasting feminism festivals film / video finance First Amendment food food banks food security foreign policy framing free speech freedom of information fundraising gambling gardening Gays genetic engineering genocide gentrification global community global issues global warming globalization government grants / financial aid Great Britain Greece greens Guatemala guns Gypsies Haiti harm reduction hate crimes health healthcare access hemp history Holocaust homelessness homeowners associations homophobia hospitals housing human rights humanism humanitarian aid humor hunger imagism immigrants impeachment imperialism incarceration India indigenous people indigenous rights individuals Indonesia initiatives insurance intellectual property intentional communities interconnectedness international law internationalism Internet intervention investigative journalism investment Iran Iranian Americans Iraq Ireland Israel Israelis Ivory Coast janitorial work Japan Japanese Americans Jewish Americans Jews journalism judiciation justice juvenile justice Korean Americans Kurds labor labor councils labor union locals land reform land trusts land use landmines Latin America Latinas / Latinos law lawyers lead poisoning leadership development leafleting legal defense legal services legislation Lesbians letter-writing libertarianism libraries life necessities limits to economic growth literacy litigation living wage lobbying local currencies local economy local food long-term care low-income mail-order mandatory minimum sentencing marriage rights material aid Mayans media media criticism mediation medical marijuana men mental health mentoring Mexico microbroadcasting microenterprise micropower Middle East militarism military occupation military recruitment militias minimum wage mining multiculturalism multiple chemical sensitivity Mumia Abu-Jamal municipal government murals museums music Muslims Myanmar NAFTA / GATT / FTAA national government nationalism Native Americans needle exchange neighborhoods neoliberalism networking news news on-line newsletters newspapers Nicaragua Nigeria noise pollution noncorporate economy nonviolence North America North Korea nuclear energy nuclear radiation nuclear weapons / testing nudism nursing homes nutrition OCCUPY occupational safety and health offshoring jobs open government open space organic agriculture orphans outdoor activity ozone Pacific Islands Pakistan Palestinians Panama parks patents PATRIOT Act peace peace centers peak oil pedestrian advocacy people of color performance art permaculture Peru pesticides petitions petroleum petroleum-rich nations Philippines / Filipinos philosophy physician-assisted suicide picketing places plastic police accountability policy Political Action Committees (PACs) political parties political prisoners pollution population control populism pornography posters and flyers poverty prevention printers prisons privacy private government privatization products propaganda property rights proportional representation psychotherapy public education public health Puerto Rico punk racism radio radioactivity rainforests rape recycling refugees relationships religion religious right renewable energy rent control reparations reproductive rights researchers retreats reuse right to know right-wingers Romanis runaways rural life Russia sacred sites Saudi Arabia School of the Americas science secession seeds self-defense self-determination self-help self-reliance selfsufficiency seniors separation of church and state services sex sex trafficking sex work sexism sexual harassment sexual minorities shareholder advocacy sharing shelters simple living single payer health care sister communities sizism skepticism slavery socialism socioeconomic models software solar energy solidarity South Africa South America South Asian Americans South Korea spirituality spoken word sports spying squatting Sri Lanka state government stem cell research street theater strikes students study groups Sudan suicide prevention sunshine laws support groups surveillance sustainability sweatshops taxes technology television temp work tenant rights terrorism textiles Thailand think tanks Tibet tobacco torture tourism toxics trade transgenders transportation trees Turkey United Nations unity urban life urban planning urban sprawl utilities veganism / vegetarianism Venezuela veterans Vietnam vigils violence vivisection volunteer matching voter registration waste watchdog groups water watersheds welfare wetlands whistleblowing wilderness wildlife women World Bank / IMF world government World Trade Organization yoga youth Yugoslavia Zapatistas Zimbabwe

INTERVIEW NOTES

Some of my favorite moments in life were when I sat in rooms with community activists, volunteers, or nonprofit workers, tape recorder in hand, asking what inspired them to engage. You will find their stories throughout this book. They spoke about the strong desire to contribute, about not knowing how to get started, or of finding themselves in unusual circumstances in which they suddenly were swept into action. Some took part in extraordinary moments in our recent history: fighting apartheid in South Africa, organizing in San Francisco's gay rights movement, showing up at protests on climate change.

At the beginning of each chapter I've shared stories and observations from some of them.

Week 1: Adrienne Shall and Sue Lieberman

Week 2: Marcus

Week 3: Dennis Seeley and Gwenn Craig

Week 4: Alberto Saldamando, Joanna Macy and Louise Dunlap

Week 5: Dennis Seeley and Gwenn Craig

Week 6: Julie Pokrivnak and Jim Bates

Week 7: Joanna Macy and Louise Dunlap

Week 8: Tempel Smith

Adrienne Shall and Sue Lieberman. At the time of the interview Adrienne worked for the Institute for a Democratic Alternative for South Africa and Sue was a community development consultant.

"Marcus" was an activist in Cape Town, South Africa and later a civil society sector consultant. He requested anonymity.

Dennis Seely and Gwenn Craig met in the San Francisco Castro district back in the mid-seventies when a gay social justice movement was blossoming. Their shared experience spanned nude beaches and campaigning out of Harvey Milk's camera store. I would call them lifelong activists, except that Dennis would likely dispute any kind of label. During the interview both spoke often and with nostalgia of their friend Bill Krauss, who was a political force for gay rights and who died of AIDS in the mid-eighties. "He embodied the idea of you want to change the system and you wanna have fun too," Dennis said.

Alberto Saldamando has been a human rights attorney, public interest advocate, activist, executive director, and Peace Corps volunteer in Lesotho. He worked for seventeen years as general counsel for the International Indian Treaty Council (IITC) and currently works for the Indigenous Environmental Network.

Joanna Macy and Louise Dunlap: Joanna is a renowned Buddhist ecologist, thinker, and teacher. She is the author of several books, including *World as Lover, World as Self*. Grounded in Buddhist teachings, her writing and workshops help people consciously experience their pain and compassion for the world. Her most recent books are *Active Hope* and an update of her classic *Coming Back to Life*. Louise, a writing teacher and veteran of the Berkeley Free Speech Movement, wrote *Undoing the Silence*, a book packed with exercises to help free and hone the words of those writing for social change.

Julie Pokrivnak is a schoolteacher in Hayward, California, and has volunteered for many nonprofits, including the National Organization for Women and the American Civil Liberties Union.

Jim Bates is a facilities caretaker at Spirit Rock Meditation Center, a budding poet, and a hospice volunteer.

Tempel Smith is a Buddhist meditation teacher with a background in service and activism centered on nuclear disarmament, environmental protection, and working in crisis shelters for homeless and abused youth. He also founded a residential community dedicated to living a socially engaged Buddhist life.

REFERENCES

Alda, Alan. *Never Have Your Dog Stuffed*. Random House, 2005.

Alinsky, Saul. *Rules for Radicals*. Random House, 1971.

American Psychological Association Task Force on the Interface Between Psychology and Global Climate Change. "Psychology and Global Climate Change: Addressing a Multi-faceted Phenomenon and Set of Challenges" (2010). change-booklet.pdf.

Amodeo, John. "Focusing: Connecting to Our Soul Through Feelings." *Share Guide* (November, 2003).

Barasch, Marc Ian. *Field Notes on the Compassionate Life: A Search for the Soul of Kindness*. Rodale, 2005.

Blaustein, Arthur. *Make a Difference: Your Guide to Volunteering and Community Service*. Heyday Books, 2002.

Bornstein, Arthur. *How to Change the World: Social Entrepreneurs and the Power of New Ideas*. Oxford University Press, 2007.

Brach, Tara. *Embracing Your Life with the Heart of a Buddha*. Bantam Books, 2003.

Bronson, Po. *What Should I Do with My Life?: The True Story of People Who Answered the Ultimate Question*. Random House, 2002.

Brown, Jerry. *Dialogues*. Berkeley Hills Books, 1998.

Butterfly Hill, Julia. *One Makes the Difference: Inspiring Actions that Change Our World*. Harper San Francisco, 2002

Cameron, Julia. *The Artist's Way*. Penguin Putnam, 1992.

Coates, Ta-Nehisi. *Between the World and Me.* Spiegel & Grau, 2015.

Cohen, Robert and Reginald E. Zelnik, eds. *The Free Speech Movement: Reflections on Berkeley in the 1960s.* University of California Press, 2002.

Corporation for National and Community Service, Office of Research and Policy. The Health Benefits of Volunteering: A Review of Recent Research (2007). www.nationalservice.gov/pdf/07_0506_hbr.pdf.

H. H. The Dalai Lama. *Ethics for the New Millennium.* Riverhead, 1999.

Dass, Ram and Paul Gorman. *How Can I Help?: Stories and Reflections on Service.* Alfred A. Knopf, 1985.

Dass, Ram and Mirabai Bush. *Compassion in Action: Setting Out on the Path of Service.* Three Rivers Press, 1995.

Davis, Belva. *Never in My Wildest Dreams: A Black Woman's Life in Journalism.* Berrett-Koehler (2011).

De Tocqueville, Alexis. *Democracy in America.* Originally published as De la Démocratie en Amérique in two parts (1835, 1840), reprint: Anchor Books, 1969.

Dominguez, Joseph R. and Vicki Robin. *Your Money or Your Life: Transforming Your Relationship with Money and Achieving Financial Independence.* Viking Penguin, 1992.

Dunlap, Louise. *Undoing the Silence: Six Tools for Social Change Writing.* New Village Press, 2006.

Ellsberg, Daniel. *Secrets: A Memoir of Vietnam and the Pentagon Papers.* Viking, 2002.

Pope Francis. "Encyclical Letter Laudato si' of the Holy Father Francis on Care for Our Common Home" (2015).

Frankl, Viktor E. *Man's Search for Meaning: An Introduction to Logotherapy.* Originally published 1959. Fourth edition: Beacon Press, 1992.

Fromm, Erich. *The Art of Loving.* Originally published 1956. Reprint: Thorsons, 1995.

Goldberg, Natalie. *Writing Down the Bones.* Shambhala, 1986.

Goleman, Daniel. *Emotional Intelligence.* Bantam Books, 1995.

Greenwald, Glen. Speech (via Skype) on Edward Snowden to the Socialism 2013 conference in Chicago on June 27, 2013. Video. wearemany.org/v/2013/06/glenn-greenwald-speaks-out.

Hawken, Paul. *Blessed Unrest: How the Largest Social Movement in History Is Restoring Grace, Justice, and Beauty to the World.* Viking Penguin, 2007.

hooks, bell. *All about Love: New Visions.* William Morrow, 1999.

Horton, Myles. *The Long Haul: An Autobiography.* Doubleday, 1990.

Kelly, Petra. *Thinking Green! Essays on Environmentalism, Feminism, and Nonviolence.* Parallax Press, 1994.

Klein, Naomi. *This Changes Everything: Capitalism vs. the Climate.* Simon and Schuster, 2014.

Kristof, Nicholas D. and Sheryl WuDunn. *A Path Appears: Transforming Lives, Creating Opportunity.* Alfred Knopf, 2014.

Lamott, Anne. *Bird by Bird: Some Instructions on Writing and Life.* Anchor Books, 1995.

Lappé, Francis Moore and Jeffrey Perkins. *You Have the Power: Choosing Courage in a Culture of Fear.* Penguin, 2004.

Lipsky, Laura van Dernoot. *Trauma Stewardship: An Everyday Guide to Caring for Self While Caring for Others.* Berrett-Koehler, 2009.

Loeb, Paul Rogat. *Soul of a Citizen: Living with Conviction in a Cynical Time.* St. Martin's Griffin, 1999.

Loeb, Paul Rogat. *The Impossible Will Take a Little While: Perseverance and Hope in Troubled Times.* Basic Books, 2014.

Macy, Joanna and Molly Brown. *Coming Back to Life: The Updated Guide to The Work that Reconnects.* New Society Publishers, 2014.

Mandela, Nelson. *Long Walk to Freedom.* Abacus, 1995.

McKay, Matthew, Martha Davis, and Patrick Fanning. *How to Communicate: The Ultimate Guide to Improving Your Personal and Professional Relationships.* MJF Books, 1993.

Neff, Kristin. *Self-Compassion: The Proven Power of Being Kind to Yourself.* William Morrow, 2011.

Nhat Hanh, Thich. *Anger: Wisdom for Cooling the Flames.* Riverhead, 2001.

Nisker, Wes. *You are Not Your Fault and Other Revelations.* Soft Skull Press, 2016.

Nyathi, Andrew. *Tomorrow Is Built Today.* Anvil Press, 1990.

Parker, Ian. "The Gift: Zell Kravinsky Gave Away Millions but Somehow It Wasn't Enough." *The New Yorker* (Aug. 2, 2004).

Peace Pilgrim. *Peace Pilgrim: Her Life and Work in Her Own Words.* Ocean Tree Books, 1983.

Pipher, Mary. *The Green Boat: Reviving Ourselves in Our Capsized Culture.* Riverhead, 2013.

Rosenberg, Marshall B. *Nonviolent Communication: A Language of Compassion.* PuddleDancer Press, 2002.

Rothberg, Donald. *The Engaged Spiritual Life: A Buddhist Approach to Transforming Ourselves and the World.* Beacon Press, 2006.

Roy, Arundhati. "What Shall We Love?" *Outlook* (Nov. 26, 2015).

Salmon, Jaqueline L. "Most Americans Believe in a Higher Power, Poll Finds." *The Washington Post* (June 24, 2008).

Snapp, Martin. "Free Speech at 40." *Contra Costa Times,* (Nov. 28, 2004).

Solnit, Rebecca. *A Paradise Built in Hell: The Extraordinary Communities That Arise in Disaster.* Viking, 2009

The South End Press Collective, ed. *Talking About a Revolution: Interviews with Michael Albert, Noam Chomsky, Barbara Ehrenreich, bell hooks, Peter Kwong, Winona LaDuke, Manning Marable, Urvashi Vaid, and Howard Zinn.* South End Press, 2008.

Terkel, Studs. *Hope Dies Last: Keeping the Faith in Difficult Times.* The New Press, 2003.

Terkel, Studs. *Working.* Avon Books, 1972.

Vassallo, Wanda. *Speaking with Confidence: A Guide for Public Speakers.* Betterway Publications, 1990.

Weddady, Nasser and Sohrab Ahmari, eds. *Arab Spring Dreams: The Next Generation Speaks Out for Freedom and Justice from North Africa to Iran.* St. Martin's Press, 2012.

Zinn, Howard. "Against Discouragement." Commencement address at Spelman College (May 15, 2005).

tamejavifellows.wordpress.com/2016/07/22/call-to-peace.

www.tomdispatch.com/post/2728/graduation_day_with_howard_zinn.

www.theguardian.com/teacher-network/2012/aug/19/why-i-became-a-teacher.

www.yourclassical.org/story/2015/05/01/black-lives-matter.

Acknowledgements

I want to thank everyone who shared their stories and who ultimately made it impossible for me not to finish this workbook (which has turned out to be a very long, slow, step by step undertaking indeed). This is your book too.

I want to start by thanking the many people who were kind enough to share through formal interviews. Thank you for your candor, wisdom, humor, and heart, not to mention all the ways you have contributed and continue to make positive change in the world: Adrienne Shall, Sue Lieberman, Neil Nair, Jerome Friedman, Fiona Archer, Anton Eberhard, Kallie Hanekom, "Marcus," Ntobeko Ngalo, Raymond Shuller, Alberto Saldamando, Isao Fujimoto, Gwenn Craig, Dennis Seely, Andy Buckley Bramble, Pramod Daya, Julie Pokrivnak, Mike Adams, Miki Kashtan, Sue King, Shiloh Barnat, Greg Beuthin, Catherine Miller, Jon Jackson, Louise Dunlap, Joanna Macy, Tempel Smith, Robert Cusick, Tim Andres, Jim Bates, and Bing Gong.

Thank you to those who encouraged me in so many practical and emotionally supportive ways, most especially the Pentavera women–Joslyn Grieve, Paula Baker, Elizabeth Rudd, and Karen Nyhus–and to Natasha Haugnes; Louise Dunlap's Friday morning writing group; my mom, Mary Nelson, and step-dad, John Ferreira; James Baraz; Susan Orr; Wes Nisker; Linda Jaskol; Josh Senyak; Karen Nordback; Naomi Elvove; Cindy Davis and Todd Pickering; Beth Baker; Betsy and John Griffith; Kathy Cheney; Quilley Powers; Mary Ellen Braly; Laurie and Gail Goldman; Ashley Sharpe; Rosemary Nelson; Geoff Minshull Kirsten Wildefang; Rachel Levy Bencheton; Rachael Riley; Rachel Humphreys; Jim Rogers; Gabriele Schwibach; Regula Keller; Vig Swaminathan; Carl Strasen and the Spirit Rock community.

Thanks to the editors and book advisors who helped me get this out in the end: especially to Louise Dunlap (who wrote a great book, *Undoing the Silence: Six Tools for Social Change Writing*) and also to Sam Barry at Book Passage (co-author of the helpful *Write that Book Already!*), Mark Burstein, Carla King and Margaret Wylie.

And, for her inspiring and almost uncannily complementary artwork, thanks to artist extraordinaire Anna Oneglia.

About the Author

Kerry Nelson grew up in San Francisco, and graduated from Peace and Conflict Studies and Library and Information Studies from UC Berkeley. Inspired by social justice movements, for two decades she consulted, volunteered and advocated with non-profits, unions, and individuals in the U.S., southern Africa and the U.K. She currently works as a retreat manager at Spirit Rock Meditation Center, advocates for action on climate change, and offers *One Small Difference* and *One Small Planet* workshops. Visit her at placeforpeace.org to learn more.

Lightning Source UK Ltd.
Milton Keynes UK
UKOW03f2004300317

297940UK00004B/288/P